Weather Reports from
the Autism Front

ALSO BY JAMES C. WILSON
AND FROM McFARLAND

---

*The Hawthorne and Melville Friendship:
An Annotated Bibliography, Biographical and
Critical Essays, and Correspondence Between the Two* (1991)

John Reed for The Masses (1987)

Vietnam in Prose and Film (1982)

Weather Reports from the Autism Front

A Father's Memoir of His Autistic Son

JAMES C. WILSON

McFarland & Company, Inc., Publishers
Jefferson, North Carolina, and London

LIBRARY OF CONGRESS CATALOGUING-IN-PUBLICATION DATA

Wilson, James C., 1948–
Weather reports from the autism front : a father's memoir
of his autistic son / James C. Wilson.
p.   cm.
Includes bibliographical references and index.

ISBN 978-0-7864-3705-4
softcover : 50# alkaline paper ∞

1. Wilson, Sam — Mental health.   2. Wilson, James C., 1948–
3. Autistic youth — Biography.   4. Parents of autistic children —
Biography.   I. Title.
RJ506.A9W497   2008
618.92'858820092 — dc22   2007051489
[B]

British Library cataloguing data are available

On the cover: Sam Wilson waves at the camera after planting
his backpack, reclaiming his beach, and setting up shop, with his
portable CD player, South Beach, December 2006.

Manufactured in the United States of America

*McFarland & Company, Inc., Publishers
Box 611, Jefferson, North Carolina 28640
www.mcfarlandpub.com*

Acknowledgments

Many people deserve special thanks for helping me with this book.

I am grateful for the advice, early on, of literary agent Jane Chelius and editors Colleen Sell and Ladette Randolph.

Thanks to my friends and colleagues working in the exciting academic field of Disability Studies. I've enjoyed working and exchanging ideas with so many of them, especially Michael Berube, Brenda Brueggemann, Tom Couser, Lenny Davis, David Mitchell, and Sharon Snyder. Also, thanks to all the members of the Society for Disability Studies and Disability Studies in the Humanities list-servs. I only wish I could be more active on the lists.

I would also like to thank all the autistic bloggers I have quoted in this book. I've learned much from their insight, wisdom, and courage.

I am grateful to the University of Cincinnati for granting me the academic leave that allowed me to write this book.

Finally, I would like to thank my life partner, Cynthia Lewiecki-Wilson, whom I can never repay for her love, her great ideas, and her patience with me on our collaborative projects.

Contents

Contents

"Tragically, as many as 9,625 out of every 10,000 individuals may be neurotypical."

— *Institute for the Study of the Neurologically Typical*

Preface

Sometimes you just have to laugh. Take this morning, for example. I'm sitting at my kitchen table reading a newspaper when my 26-year-old son walks into the room listening to his portable CD player. He has the headphones squashed down over his baseball cap and the wires tangled around his neck. His jeans hang low on his hips, but underneath he has his underwear pulled up over his navel. I know he's listening to his new Ludacris CD when he hip-hops over to the table and asks, "What's a money maker? Do I have a money maker?"

"Yep. If it means what I think it means."

"Good!" Sam says proudly.

On a good day lots of words come to mind when describing Sam: goofy, witty, funny, happy, playful, cheerful, autistic. I include autistic with these other words because it's just that, a word, an adjective. Autistic is not who Sam is, it's one descriptor among many. To understand Sam, you have to spend time with him. Sit with him, listen to his music, answer his repetitive weather questions. Forget your preconceived ideas about autism, about what autistic people can and can't do. Just be with him. Enjoy him for who he is instead of seeing him for what he's not.

On a bad day a different set of adjectives come to mind.

Sometimes when we're out on the town, a well-intentioned stranger will come up and say "what a shame" or "God bless." I nod politely and walk away, not bothering to tell them what I really think of their pity. Whatever Sam is, he's not a shame, a tragedy, a joy, a test, or a gift from God. He's just Sam, a young man with a wicked sense of humor and a zest for life that those who make these condescending comments would do well to emulate.

Sam loves to greet people with a joke. He'll walk up to someone he knows and say, "I saw you last night." When the person asks where, Sam answers, "On America's Most Wanted," the television show.

During the recent election, Sam would approach his friends and say, "You suck! This is Sam Wilson, and I approve of this message."

That's the Sam I know, not the assumptions and projections of others.

Not to be overly critical, because I had to overcome my own projections, my own assumptions about autism in order to "see" Sam. When I was younger I could never have written this book. Over the years I've learned from Sam and from other autistic people. My education has taken the form of conversations, e-mail, online discussion groups, and blogs posted by auties and aspies, as autistic people sometimes refer to themselves.

If you want a wake-up call, a slap in the face, take a look at the blogs of autism activists like Zilari, Joel Smith, Autism Diva, Amanda Baggs, Elmindreda, Kassiane Montana, and the Autistic Bitch from Hell. Blogs like these will make you rethink your attitudes and readjust your priorities. My advice: listen to autistic people themselves, not to the generalizations of non-autistic run advocacy organizations whose rhetoric more often than not reinforces the social stigma attached to autism. Autism Diva's advice to parents: "STOP whining like you have it the worst of anyone." Look at us! Listen to us!

So let this be a warning to the reader. If you're looking for sentimentality, or if you want a heart-warming story about a cute, cuddly autistic child, you won't find it here. Instead, I offer a realistic account of life with an autistic adult.

Likewise, if you want a narrative of overcoming, you best look elsewhere. There are no heroes here, no supercrip savant overcoming all odds to solve the latest mystery in numbers theory, and certainly no superdad, long-suffering and self-sacrificing.

But if you like to laugh, if you're interested in the misadventures of an autistic young man trying to find his place in the world, and if you have a taste for irreverence and dark humor, welcome aboard!

Welcome, that is, to weather reports from the autism front, Sam Wilson meteorologist.

Chapter 1

The Family Gangsta

My son Sam and I have reached a standoff of sorts, an uneasy accommodation. I understand him, more or less; and he understands me, more or less. We spend far too much time together, and because of that we sometimes get tired of each other. As often as I complain about the difficulty of being the primary companion of an autistic 26-year-old, he complains about the difficulty — and boredom — of having to put up with a 58-year-old assistant. "I'm tired of you," he'll say. "You're too old for me."

Call it a hard-fought truce.

Still, I'm a realist. I've spent too much time on the psych ward to fool myself into thinking that the bad old times won't come again. Autism can't be cured or outgrown. Just last year Sam could be quietly reading the phone book one moment and then BAM, I look up and he's banging his head against the wall. Sometimes not even listening to music or watching the weather channel would calm his turbulent mind. The forecast might remain unchanged from one 15-minute segment to the next, but not Sam. Some subtle, imperceptible change in intonation or camera angle would set off a chain reaction. Serotonin would surge, dopamine receptors would tweak, and suddenly all hell would break loose. Without warning, Sam would rush through the house smashing and head-banging everything in range, looking for ... me? Yikes!

Let me be blunt. I've found that when all else fails and heads start banging, only dark humor can help me cope. I've earned my right to be sardonic. I've been punched, kicked, scratched and bitten. I've been pushed down stairs and shoved into walls. One day I suffered the indignity of being chased around my front yard by my broom-wielding son in full view of our neighbors. Hahaha, just Sam having a bad moment. Not to worry, really. He'll calm down in a second.

No question, Sam can be difficult. Yet, on other occasions he can be absolutely delightful, a pleasure to have as a life companion. At 5'8" he's a stocky 190 pounds with a more or less neatly trimmed beard and curly brown hair tucked under a baseball cap. In addition to autism, Sam has a mood disorder. When he's down, he'll sit slumped forward with his head listing to the right and his eyes half closed as though he were hibernating. But when he's wired, he paces around the house either humming or buzzing like a bee and tapping on walls and tables. For the past several years he's lived semi-independently in a fully equipped apartment in our basement dubbed the "Yellow Submarine" after its sunny yellow paint and a poster of the Beatles' movie of the same name hanging on the wall. His three other companions, all males, spend time in Sam's bachelor pad and take him out to movies and restaurants.

Unlike many people on the autism spectrum, Sam chatters nonstop about his favorite topics. His current obsessions are severe weather, especially tornadoes, and rap music, courtesy of his youngest companion who introduced Sam to the likes of Jay-Z, Snoop Dogg, Busta Rhymes, Outkast, Dr. Dre, Ludacris, 50 Cent, Jurassic 5, and the ever popular NWA. Sam and rap are a perfect fit. He loves the word play and the repetitive, pounding rhythms. Thanks to his friend, appropriately nicknamed Party Dawg, Sam has gone gangsta.

Now Sam comes hip-hopping down the hallway singing along with his headphones: "Drop it like it's hot! Drop it like it's hot!" Or "Bust a move! Bust a move!"

Sam walks the walk and talks the Rap. "Wassup?" he'll ask, when he hasn't seen me for all of five minutes. Or he'll tell me he's feeling "all eaten up" when he's not quite himself. "Hook me up," he'll say, when he wants something, usually food. He introduces his friends as his "homies." Sometimes he'll go back and forth between rap talk and weather talk, as though he's engaging in parallel conversations. Just what the world needs: a playa with an obsessive-compulsive interest in meteorology.

Sam doesn't work; he has never been able to hold down a job, partly because of the kinds of jobs people have offered him. Once in high school he was told by a job counselor to break down boxes since that was all someone with "reduced potential" could possibly do. Then after high school he was sent to a sheltered workshop and told to put screws in a box for 24 cents an hour. It would be hard to imagine a task less suited for a person who has problems with concentration, sensory overload, and fine motor coordination but who has above average intelligence. Not surprisingly, Sam refused to cooperate with his job counselors, acted up and got sent to the showers.

So instead of working, Sam recreates. But enough telling, let me show you Sam in action. Recently, Sam's social club, which caters to young adults with various disabilities, sponsored a special outing, a first ever Boy's Night Out. Where does our fearless outing leader, Tim, decide to take us? To Hooters, of course. And not just any Hooters, but the fancy marina-style Hooters on the Ohio River in downtown Cincinnati.

Everyone arrives early, ready to party. Together, we're a rainbow of ages, ethnicities, and disabilities. Sam and the other members of his club walk across the wooden ramp one at a time, accompanied by a couple of the fathers who serve as helpers, myself included. We don't have to worry about fitting in at Hooters. We're not the weirdest dudes here. None of the other customers even notices us. Not the group of Japanese businessmen, not the two grungers wearing heavy metal T-shirts, not the single guy pretending to be reading a newspaper, and certainly not the old geezers sitting at the bar nursing their beers. They're much too busy ogling the Hooters girls to care about a few extraordinary young men limping and shuffling across the wooden floor. The server girls are wearing their standard-issue tight shorts and tighter orange tops. The classy look.

7

"Man — this beats last month's outing," says one of our troops when he spots his first Hooters babe.

"I take care of my guys," says Tim, our fearless leader, a stocky young man with shoulder length brown hair. Tim plays in a rock band and appears absolutely unflappable. Nothing ruffles Tim's feathers as he supervises his group: John jumping up and down at the table, Eric scribbling in his notebook left to right, then top to bottom, and Sam asking repeatedly about tornadoes. Just another night for City Club, a social club for young people with disabilities sponsored by the United Way. Our version of "normal." Whatever normal means.

Unable to attain Tim's Zen-like state of unflappability, I keep worrying that one of our charges will reach out and grab a handful of Hooters flesh. My bad. Ironically, our guys are less distracted by Hooters babes than the other customers. Mostly, we want spicy chicken wings, platters of fries, and a round of drinks, thank you very much. Sure, we enjoy the sexy costumes, but the girls represent only one item on our party platter and definitely not the main course. We're here to party, not to ogle. We don't get out all that often. As you can probably guess, our social calendars aren't very full. But when we do go out on the town, watch out. Let the good times roll!

And for not ogling, the Hooters girls love us. Sure, we're a little strange, but at least we're not sexist pigs. No boorish behavior coming from our table. Just John, the youngest of our group, who is largely nonverbal, bouncing in his seat saying "Hi!" over and over again. So the girls hover around us two and three at a time. They can't resist our charm, like a burst of orange butterflies fluttering around our flowers. And who can blame them? How often does a group of young, distinctive, well-behaved gentlemen appear among Hooters usual clientele?

We're about to order when Eric, a young man about Sam's age, turns to his server and asks, "Do you have a death ray in your mind?"

Hahaha, everyone laughs. Good one, Eric. Our server, a blond bombshell, blushes ever so slightly. She's been asked worse, no doubt. "No, I don't," she says playfully. "But I can take your order if you're ready."

Eric likes that. You bet. Everyone tries to order at the same time until our server has to raise her hand high, like an umpire calling time out. "One at a time, boys."

When it's Sam's turn, he asks, "Which do you like better, rap or hip hop?"

"Oh," she says. "I'm not sure I know the difference?"

Sam's already on to the next topic. "Have you ever seen a tornado? Do you remember the Blue Ash tornado on April 9, 1999? Have the sirens ever gone off here?"

"Whoa," our server says. "You must like weather."

"And fire alarms," Sam adds. He reaches out and touches her bare arm lightly, then thinks twice about it and snaps his hand back. "Sorry," he says, and means it.

Sam turns to me. "Was I appropriate?" He tends to worry about his behavior — after the fact.

"Well ... you shouldn't touch, but..." I don't know how to finish my sentence.

"It's okay," our server says, all smiles.

When Sam orders, he always begins with the same question: "Which do you have, Coke or Pepsi?" Not that it matters, since whichever they have is what he orders. But Sam has to follow his ritual. His next question is: "Do you have pizza or chicken tenders?" Pizza and chicken tenders represent the staff of life for Sam. Only on rare occasions will he break his routine and order a cheeseburger, as long as the server understands that no lettuce, tomato, onion, or pickle should touch his cheeseburger. If vegetable touches burger, we're in for a bumpy ride.

"We have chicken tenders, served with lots of French fries," our server responds.

"Yeah baby. Pile it on!"

Everybody agrees. Pile it on!

When the food comes, we pounce. We might not be pretty to

watch, with stacks of extra napkins and wet wipes all around, but no one could ever accuse us of not enjoying our food.

Later, when we've pretty much finished eating, most of us bearing the telltale signs of catsup and barbecue sauce, the servers take turns coming over to visit. We've won them over with our good looks, charming behavior, and healthy appetites.

Then Andrew, our oldest, jumps up and heads for the gift counter. Someone jokes that he wants to buy a Hooters outfit for his mom. Yeah, right, wouldn't she love that? But when he returns it's with a Hooters T-shirt for himself. We all agree that Andrew will be one handsome dude in his new Hooters T-shirt. Always a ham, Andrew pulls the T-shirt over his head, eye-glasses and all, just so we can see how good he looks. He straightens his glasses and mugs for us and the ladies. Joking, one of the servers asks if he wants to work at Hooters.

Meanwhile, Sam has cornered another server. "What about the Xenia tornado of 1974? That's famous, you know. The biggest outbreak of tornadoes in recorded history."

"Really..."

"Yeah, I have a book on that one. Do you like fire alarms?"

"No, I don't like alarms. They're too loud."

"Me neither. Except for Simplex. Do you have any Simplex fire alarms here?" When she doesn't answer, Sam says, "That's okay, not everybody has a Simplex."

When we leave, it's with a sense of satisfaction, with the knowledge that we made new friends and interacted with everyone, including the Hooters girls, and that we partied to the max and left quite an impression. We have the T-shirts and catsup stains to prove it. Someone wants to know when and where Tim's rock band will be playing, so that we can continue the party, whenever. Let's do Hooters again. Why not? Hooters rules!

Sam and I are the last to leave. He's made it this far without a serious gaff. But suddenly he reaches out and takes our server's hand and looks deeply into her eyes. "If you were president, you'd be Baberaham Lincoln," he says, repeating a line from the movie *Wayne's World*.

She laughs. "Thank you — I think!"

I breathe a sigh of relief. He could have repeated his favorite line from *Austin Powers: Goldmember*. The one about shagging!

"Did I blow my cover?" he asks on the way out the door, a big grin on his face.

I have to laugh. "No, we did well."

At that Sam says, "Bust a move!" and does a hip hop dance shuffle on the deck. Then he heads for the ramp that will take him to shore, with me following along behind.

Chapter 2

Contesting Autism

Like any parent of an autistic child, I wanted to learn all I could about autism. Soon after Sam was diagnosed I did research in the library and online, looking especially at official government and organizational websites. Initially, I assumed autism resembled other disorders, with specific, well-defined causes, characteristics, and treatments. What I discovered was anything but well-defined. The more I read, the more confused I became by the dizzying array of generalizations about what autistic children can and can't do.

These official websites agreed on the most basic definition of autism: a complex developmental disorder involving brain chemistry that usually manifests by the age of three and that affects boys four times more than girls. The most recent statistics compiled by the Centers for Disease Control suggest that 1 in every 150 children will be diagnosed with an Autism Spectrum Disorder. The Autism Society of America, which calls itself "the voice of the autism community" (a claim that is rejected by many autistic bloggers and advocates), argues that autism is "the result of a neurological disorder that affects the normal functioning of the brain, impacting development in the areas of social interaction and communication skills." Most prominent on the ASA homepage, as others have pointed out, is the pitch for viewers to join ASA and make a financial contribution.

The word "normal" appears frequently on the ASA and other official websites, as if that word actually meant anything. What's normal? To whom? Fact is, the meaning of the word normal is not a given, is not evident. Far from it. The meaning of normal depends on a context, a frame of reference that has to be costructed. And who does the constructing? People.

If you think about it, you'll find that normal is a slippery slope. What's normal to me might not be normal to you. Actually, I'm not sure that any of my extended family would be considered normal under any definition of the word.

But my favorite statement on the ASA website, under the "Living with Autism" heading, offers advice to parents on how to cope: "The demands of raising a child with autism are great, and families frequently experience high levels of stress. Recognizing and preparing yourself for the challenges that are in store will make a tremendous difference to all involved, including the parents, siblings, grandparents, extended family, and friends." Stress? Challenges? You think? And as far as finding siblings, grandparents, extended family, and friends who want to be involved with Sam, I'm still looking.

Autism Speaks, another nonprofit website co-founded by Suzanne and Bob Wright, adds the following: "Autism impairs a person's ability to communicate and relate to others. It is also associated with rigid routines and repetitive behaviors, such as obsessively arranging objects or following very specific routines. Symptoms can range from very mild to quite severe."

That is, autism is a spectrum disorder that includes a wide variety of symptoms, behaviors, and abilities. This variety makes it extremely difficult to predict outcomes and just about impossible to foretell the future of any particular person affected. Autism spectrum disorders range from so-called "Higher Functioning" to so-called "Lower Functioning" in this order: Asperger's Syndrome, Pervasive Developmental Disability, Autism, Childhood Disintegrative Disorder, and Rett's Disorder. The movie *Rain Man* popularized Asperger's Syndrome, which is often associated with savant skills in math, music, and art.

Temple Grandin, who has Asperger's, has become something of a national spokesperson for the disorder. Grandin teaches Animal

Science at Colorado State University and has written several books on autism. Some of her theories comparing the way autistic people learn to the way animals learn have not been well received in the larger autism community.

The Centers for Disease Control in Atlanta, Georgia, describes autism spectrum disorders as a "group of developmental disabilities defined by significant impairments in social interaction and communication and the presence of unusual behaviors and interests. Many people with ASDs also have unusual ways of learning, paying attention, or reacting to different sensations."

Okay. Unusual behaviors and interests. Unusual ways of learning and paying attention. Again, the generalizations don't have much predictive power in the individual case. I didn't need the CDC to tell me that Sam exhibits unusual behaviors and interests. So do I, for that matter.

What causes autism? The official websites tend to agree that a complex interaction of genetic and environmental factors triggers autism. The CDC website makes the case most succinctly: "Family studies have shed the most light on the genetic contribution to autism. Studies of twins have shown that in identical twins there is about a 75 percent rate of both twins having autism, while in non-identical twins this occurs about 3 percent of the time. The inheritance pattern is complex and suggests that a number of genes are involved."

The CDC lists other factors associated with an increased risk of autism, including medical conditions such as Fragile X syndrome, tuberous sclerosis, congenital rubella syndrome, and untreated phenylketonuria (PKU). The Center for the Study of Autism in Salem, Oregon, adds another category to their list of associated risk factors: viruses. They include the cytolomegalo virus and certain viruses associated with vaccines, especially the MMR vaccine. This last comes as something of a surprise, since most official websites discredit the vaccination conspiracy theory supported, primarily, by parent groups.

However, the vaccination theory may be revisited after the U.S.

Congress passed the 2006 Combating Autism Act. Cure Autism Now, another nonprofit advocacy group, successfully lobbied for the Act, which was signed into law by George W. Bush on Dec. 19, 2006. The Act will increase funding for autism-related research at the National Institutes of Health from $101 million in 2006 to $132 million this year and to $210 million by 2011. Among other initiatives, the NIH plans to investigate the possible role of neuro-toxic compounds such as pesticides and mercury in causing autism.

Most cases of autism are diagnosed by the age of three or four, according to official websites. Early signs of autism include not speaking, gesturing, or making eye contact by 18 months of age, as well as repetitive speech or actions. The Cure Autism Now website adds the following sign: "Unusual reactions to the way things look, feel, smell, taste or sound." Unusual reactions? Okay.

Official criteria for diagnosing autism can be found in the *Diagnostic and Statistical Manual of Mental Disorders*, published and updated periodically by the American Psychiatric Association. The current edition, the *DSM IV TR,* groups diagnostic criteria into three general categories: social interaction, communication, and repetitive and stereotyped patterns of behavior. But to diagnose a patient using the *DSM IV TR* criteria, a medical professional has to first engage in a little mixing and matching. Let's take a look at how this rather clumsy diagnostic instrument actually works.

A diagnosis of "Autistic Disorder" requires a medical professional to identify, "A total of six (or more) items from (1), (2), and (3), with at least two from (1), and one each from (2) and (3):"

1. qualitative impairment in social interaction, as manifested by at least two of the following:
   - marked impairment in the use of multiple nonverbal behaviors such as eye-to-eye gaze, facial expression, body postures, and gestures to regulate social interaction.
   - failure to develop peer relationships appropriate to developmental level.
   - a lack of spontaneous seeking to share enjoyment, interests,

15

or achievements with other people (e.g., by a lack of showing, bringing, or pointing out objects of interest).
- lack of social or emotional reciprocity.

2. qualitative impairments in communication as manifested by at least one of the following:
   - delay in, or total lack of, the development of spoken language (not accompanied by an attempt to compensate through alternative modes of communication such as gesture or mime).
   - in individuals with adequate speech, marked impairment in the ability to initiate or sustain a conversation with others.
   - stereotyped and repetitive use of language or idiosyncratic language.
   - lack of varied, spontaneous make-believe play or social imitative play appropriate to developmental level.

3. restricted repetitive and stereotyped patterns of behavior, interests, and activities, as manifested by at least one of the following:
   - encompassing preoccupation with one or more stereotyped and restricted patterns of interest that is abnormal either in intensity or focus.
   - apparently inflexible adherence to specific, nonfunctional routines or rituals.
   - stereotyped and repetitive motor manners (e.g., hand or finger flapping or twisting, or complex whole-body movements).
   - persistent preoccupation with parts of objects.

To the above, the *DSM IV TR* adds the following two items:

First, delays or abnormal functioning in at least one of the following areas, with onset prior to age 3 years: (1) social interaction, (2) language as used in social communication, or (3) symbolic or imaginative play.

Second, the disturbance is not better accounted for by Rett's Disorder or Childhood Disintegrative Disorder (separate diagnostic criteria for these and the other disorders on the Autism Spectrum are included in the *DSM IV TR*).

Considered separately, each of the above criteria seems reasonable enough, if predictable. It's the mixing and matching that I find problematic. What if I present with only five items (instead of six) from categories (1), (2) and (3)? Can I be diagnosed with autism disorder? Or if I present with only one item (instead of two) from category (1), but two items from categories (2) and (3)? Or just one item from each of the three categories? You see my point. As a diagnostic tool, the mixing and matching seems overly fluid, even arbitrary.

In addition, the criteria strike me as overly general or, in the language of the *DSM IV TR*, stereotyped. For example, virtually every adolescent male I knew growing up in my small Midwestern town had problems with social interaction, communication, and repetitive behaviors. We weren't very social, we didn't talk much, and we would spend hour after hour engaged in repetitive activities such as throwing a baseball against a wall or shooting hoops. Every day, inside or outside, we would repeat the same activities, without much interaction or communication. According to *the DSM IV TR*, we might have been diagnosed with autism disorder. My point here is that the criteria are so general that any diagnosis comes down to a judgment call. An opinion.

Every official website includes a list of possible behaviors that characterize autistic people. They fall into five main categories. The first category involves perseverative, repetitive, and self-stimulating behaviors, such as rocking, clapping, tapping, and hand flapping. The second category consists of self-injurious behaviors, such as biting, head-banging, and pulling out hair. The third category involves asocial behaviors, including not interacting, making eye contact, or understanding the feelings of others. The fourth category contains a range of sensory sensitivities, such as painful aversion to noise, crowds, and being touched. Communication problems make up the fifth category. Here's the CDC on communication issues:

About 40 percent of children with ASDs do not talk at all. Others have echolalia, which is when they repeat back something that was said to them. The repeated words might be said right away or at a later time. For example, if you ask someone with an ASD, "Do you want some juice?" he or she will repeat "Do you want some juice?" instead of answering your question. Or a person might repeat a television ad heard sometime in the past.

Let's examine this statement. About 40 percent of autistic children don't talk? Can't talk? Won't talk? What exactly does this statement mean? Where does the CDC get the number 40? And what about those autistic people who communicate in different ways? Some, for example, rely on computer-mediated or facilitated communication. Many communicate by e-mail. Some even have their own blogs and hi-tech websites, complete with a sophisticated mix of text, graphics, and videos.

One of the most prolific autistic bloggers is Amanda Baggs, who launched the Getting the Truth Out website to challenge the propaganda (as she sees it) of organizations like Autism Society of America and Autism Speaks, which are not run by autistic people. She also writes an equally defiant blog, which she calls Ballastexistenz. Though incredibly articulate, Baggs does not speak; she relies on computer-mediated communication. There are many autistic people like Baggs who communicate differently but quite effectively.

Even a superstar, supercrip like Temple Grandin acknowledges that it took her a long time to learn how to talk. It wasn't that she couldn't talk; she just had to learn how. She writes in "An Inside View of Autism" that: "Not being able to speak was utter frustration. If adults spoke directly to me I could understand everything they said, but I could not get my words out. It was like a big stutter."

I found perhaps the strangest list of problem behaviors on the ASA website. Labeled the "most likely areas in which an autistic person may encounter problems with the law," the list includes the following:

- Bizarre behavior — such as severe tantrums, head-banging, and hand-flapping; these behaviors are sometimes misperceived by others as due to the influence of drugs or alcohol.

- Inappropriate social boundaries — such as approaching and/or touching strangers.
- Violating social norms — such as walking in the street, stealing, trespassing, stalking.
- Property damage — such as starting fires, throwing objects.

The ASA website goes on to say that if autistic people break the law, they should not be incarcerated but continue to receive treatment and education to control future "malfeasance."

I made a note to remember this, just in case Sam runs afoul of the law.

So what about treatment and education? How are children with autism spectrum disorders treated and educated? Again, I found a wide variety of treatments, everything from medication, to diet and nutritional supplements, to highly structured educational programs. The Autism Speaks website lists the most common interventions as Applied Behavior Analysis (ABA), Floortime Therapy, Speech Therapy, Occupational Therapy, Sensory Integration Therapy, Relationship Development Intervention, Verbal Behavior Intervention, and the school-based TEAACH method.

Of these, I have the most problem with Behavior Modification, under whatever tired guise it appears. First, the purpose of Behavior Modification is normalization, to me a problematic concept. Second, the techniques employed by Behavior Modification professionals are often brutal, self-defeating, and self-perpetuating. How long before the psycho-social community buries B.F. Skinner? I couldn't count the number of Behavior Mod programs inflicted upon Sam by well-meaning (I guess) educators who simply did not have a clue about how to reach Sam.

One example. The science teacher (and swimming coach) who declared that what Sam needed most of all was a dose of "tough love." After the physical altercation that ensued, he and Sam ended up in the principal's office. Repeatedly. I never did get a chance to ask him how that "tough love" worked for him. I know how it worked for Sam. It didn't.

Other than a basic definition of autism, the most consensus I found on these websites concerned the relatively short history of the disorder, first reported by Leo Kanner of Johns Hopkins in 1943 about the same time that a German scientist by the name of Hans Asperger described a less severe form of the disorder (Asperger's syndrome). Even so, autism as an official clinical diagnosis wasn't added to the *DSM* until 1980, when it became (so to speak) a billable, pillable disorder.

Reading these official websites provided me with a wealth of information, I'll admit. At the time I was grateful for the knowledge, but as Sam grew older I became more frustrated because none of this information helped me understand Sam as he experienced his life. More than anything, I wanted to hear autistic people talk about their lives. How they experienced the world. Yet comments from people with autism were conspicuously absent from these websites. If they were present at all, autistic people (or their photos) were used as medicalized objects to be spoken for by parents or professionals. Even on a website that calls itself Autism Speaks, we find autistic people objectified and medicalized in the most negative of terms. For example, on the "Founder's Message" page we find the following: "In 2004, our grandson was diagnosed with autism. Helpless, we watched him slip away into the cruel embrace of this disorder."

Well, I suppose, but when we frame autism in such negative terms, what effect does that have on autistic people? It's easy to understand why many autistic bloggers consider Autism Speaks a hate group (Autism Diva refers to it as "Autism Stinks," Rett Devil as "Autism Weeps"). These websites, taken as a whole, tend to reinforce the worst negative stereotypes about people with autism: that they are largely nonverbal, retarded, and lacking in imagination and social skills.

My experience with Sam and his friends told me that these stereotypes were just that: stereotypes. I'd hoped Sam could provide me with some insight into how he experienced the world. And he has, to a certain extent. Except that fathers and sons have the same kind of issues that mothers and daughters have, so that Sam sometimes can be reticent to answer my questions. He'll talk more freely with other people, including my wife, Cindy. He seems to think I'm prying where I shouldn't be prying. He's also learned over the years to be very guarded about his disabilities. Put bluntly, he resents being interrogated.

Then, several years ago, a colleague told me to check out the Autism Network International website maintained by Jim Sinclair and others at Syracuse University. ANI refers to itself as an "autistic-run self-help and advocacy organization for autistic people." From there I expanded my search and discovered, much to my delight, other websites maintained by and for autistic people. In particular, I discovered Aspies for Freedom, Autism-Vox, and Autistics.Org, which calls itself the "real voice of autism," as well as the dozens of blogs written by autistic people posted on the Autism Hub website. Using insider terms to describe themselves (as auties, aspies, autists), the Hub and other independent autistic bloggers rejected negative stereotypes about autism and challenged institutions and organizations that claimed to speak for the autistic community. Not that they were a homogeneous group with a monolithic position; they weren't. They argued and bickered with each other like any other online discussion group. But I had found what I was looking for: autistic people describing their own lives.

Frankly, I've learned more about Sam from these blogs than I have from official websites. Not that I agree with all the positions taken by the autistic bloggers, some of whom are quite militant. Still, it's utterly refreshing to find autistic people speaking for themselves. What do they write about? They write about behaviors, about communication, about sensory overload, about friends and relationships. Mostly, they write about the same things that all of us write about.

Most of these blogs reject the medical model of autism; that is, autism as disease, disorder, or pathology. Instead of the "devastating" disorder of Autism Speaks, they define autism as "neurodiversity." "Autism is a neurological difference classified as a developmental disability," writes Michelle Dawson in her Autism Crisis blog. She continues: "Autism isn't a disease ... any more than femaleness is. Autism involves neurological differences, which are basic and comprehensive." She goes on to say that "autistic neurology" isn't any more or any less valid that non-autistic neurology. In point of fact, both autistic people and neuro-typicals are able to develop, learn, progress, and achieve, though they may do so in different ways and require different kinds of help along the way.

Even more outspoken is the autistic blogger who calls himself Ventura33. Ventura33 foregrounds the political dimension of the term neurodiversity, arguing that neurodiversity is both a concept and a civil rights movement: "In its broadest usage, it is a philosophy of social acceptance and equal opportunity for all individuals whose neurology differs from the general, or neurotypical population. The term is more commonly used, however, to refer to an ongoing campaign to end prejudice and discrimination against autistic people, a group numbering at least 20 million worldwide."

For Ventura33 and other bloggers, the concept of neurodiversity equals civil rights. Why do autistic people need a civil rights movement? Because their civil rights have been taken away by parents, teachers, and the medical community. Again, Ventura33:

> For about the past half-century, mainstream society has portrayed autistics as tragically defective, lacking even self-awareness and the capacity for basic emotions. As a result of this horrific stereotype, many small children, some as young as 2 or 3 years old, have been placed in abusive institutions or abusive behavior modification programs. Dangerous antipsychotic medications are often prescribed for autistic children, although autism is not a psychosis. Many schools routinely label autistic children, even those of above-average intelligence, as mentally disabled and segregate them into special-needs classes.

Strong stuff, much of which I have to agree with. Autistic people do more often than not lose their civil rights, being placed in group homes or institutions by parents-become-guardians or social workers. The legal concept of "civil death" would seem to apply to them more than any other group of Americans. I know this from my experience with Sam. My wife and I had to become legal guardians of Sam in order to prevent him from being probated to a state institution. Even though we took away Sam's rights for the best of reasons, we still feel conflicted about our decision and hope to restore his rights (by not renewing the limited guardianship) at some point in the future. Not an easy choice, I'm afraid.

But after reading these blogs, I understand Sam's rage at all the people who have made decisions for him, without him. His rage at me, at his mother, at his former school, at the job coach who told him he had "reduced potential," at all the hectoring psychiatrists and social workers who interrogated him so many times that they all blurred into one big threatening face. Sam understands that he has certain impairments, that he needs help doing certain things, but he's also fiercely proud and wants to make his own decisions.

Will the concept of neurodiversity lead to a new acceptance of difference? Maybe, but acceptance by itself isn't enough. Most autistic people need accommodations and supports. They need aides and note-takers at school, assistants and companions at home. But let's face it, everyone (autistic or not) needs help from countless others: nurses, doctors, lawyers, personal trainers, therapists, housekeepers, gardeners, auto mechanics, electricians, plumbers, investment brokers, family members, and so on. The autonomous individual is an American myth. Needing help is not something to be ashamed of, no matter what anyone says. For autistic people the question becomes how to pay for the accommodations they need. Where would the resources come from? SSI and state Medicaid waivers (if you can find them) simply don't provide enough funds to pay for the required services. That's the issue that will have to be resolved in order for this new "civil rights movement" to succeed.

I certainly agree that autistic people have a different neurology, but I have mixed feelings about the argument that their neurology is no more or no less valid than that of neuro-typicals. I suppose, whatever valid means. But not all autism is equal; some autistic people have more self-destructive, violent behaviors than others. I don't care how you rationalize, when your autistic child begins banging his head on the wall, neurodiversity theory doesn't provide much comfort. Some behaviors are dangerous and self-destructive. Not only are these behaviors potentially fatal, they make it difficult if not impossible for autistic people to develop, learn, progress, and achieve, in the words of Michelle Dawson. Sure, head-banging and self-injury are "different," but they are in no way positive behaviors, for anyone.

On the other hand, people and organizations that perpetuate negative stereotypes do a grave disservice to autistic people and in fact reinforce the stigma attached to autism. What message does the Autism Speaks website send to its readers by including this pull quote on the "Founder's Page": "The disease has taken our children away." Says who? Organizations like Autism Speaks would do well to actually listen to autistic people who are, after all, right there with the rest of us. Our autistic children haven't been abducted by aliens. Pretending otherwise is disingenuous and harmful to the entire autistic community.

Let me end this chapter by deferring to Amanda Baggs and her Getting Out the Truth website. Her website consists of a series of black and white photos of her doing typical (for her) things: staring, lying curled up in a ball, flapping her hands. The running text condemns organizations and institutions that appropriate the images and voices of autistic people for their own political and fund-raising purposes. The purpose of Getting Out the Truth is to talk back, to correct the distortions of these organizations and institutions:

> My life has a political context and I don't want them to have the say in what words go next to pictures of people who look like me.
> Here are the words that should go with any pictures of me.
> I am not an empty shell. Nobody is.
> I am not a walking automaton devoid of anything inside me. Nobody is.
> Nobody kidnapped me. I am right here.

And:

> If the Autism Society of America were making this website, they would not mention that in the entire way she lives her life she is trying to say

"NO! This is not who or what I am! I don't want you using my image this way, I will not be portrayed as lesser, and I will not have my life medicalized this way so you can fund the elimination of autistic people from the planet."

Chapter 3

Testing Neurodiversity

The results arrived by letter: "significant behavior problems characterized by perseverative, oppositional and manipulative behaviors. Sam was noted to have a short attention span and to be verbally hyperactive." Thus read the official diagnosis of the Center for Developmental Disorders after their tester declared Sam "untestable" and kicked us out. How could they diagnose a 5-year-old they couldn't test? It's a long story.

Let's begin at the beginning. Sam was born with hydrocephalus in December 1980. For those who don't know, hydrocephalus is a condition in which cerebral-spinal fluid doesn't circulate from the brain down the spinal column but instead builds up in the brain, causing the head to swell. As a result Sam had to be "shunted" with a flexible tube implanted under his skin, with one end inserted in his head and the other in his abdominal cavity, where the fluid is absorbed by the body. Early on Sam had several surgeries to unblock his shunt, which further delayed his gross and fine motor development. He also had visual impairments, including no depth perception.

Back then, in the early 1980s, autism had just been included in the DSM as a clinical diagnosis, so evaluators were more hesitant to use that label. Instead of being labeled autistic, Sam had "autistic-like" behaviors that included repetitive, hyperactive speech. Sam would talk nonstop, usually asking the same questions over and over, like a reverse Jeopardy game-show host whose questions all concerned weather, or whatever he happened to be interested in at the moment.

Cocktail chatter, some of his doctors and preschool teachers called it. They said it was typical of people with hydrocephalus. As a wordsmith, he always had a favorite long word to use on anyone in any situation. "Indubitably!" he'd walk around saying. "Indubitably!"

To be blunt, Sam's teachers and evaluators considered him a pain in the ass to work with.

When Sam was two, a chatterbox with bushy blond hair, he would sit on the examining table and try to grab the doctor's stethoscope. Then he would repeat the word stethoscope as a way of declaring his presence. Even at that young age, he resented doctors always talking about him as though he weren't present. Today, tired of always being the passive object, the medical specimen, he gets angry and talks back loudly to the doctor, asking as many questions as he is asked and then some.

Before enrolling Sam in public school, we took him to a Center for Developmental Disorders for evaluation, intending to use the results as a way to argue for educational opportunities for Sam. Our bad. Instead of focusing on Sam's needs (visual-perceptual and motor) the Center's diagnosis stressed behavior problems: "He demonstrated difficulty with impulse control, attention span, and displayed aggressive behavior such as yelling, pinching, scratching, and pulling the evaluator's earring when frustrated. He also said 'I'm being bad' after he was reprimanded."

So how did the Center test Sam after they declared him untestable and kicked us out? Good question. It seems the evaluator popped into Sam's nearby preschool on a couple of occasions and managed to work with him just long enough to finish an evaluation. Improbably, the evaluator used a standardized (Stanford-Binet) intelligence test on a 5-year-old with visual-perceptual problems. We were dismayed, though hardly surprised, when the Center assigned Sam an IQ of 62.

The perfidy of such an arbitrary number is that it takes on a life of its own, assuming legitimacy and objectivity through repetition. Our worst fears came true when the public schools consulted the Center and came to the same conclusion: "Sammy is a five year old boy with handicaps in language pragmatics and visual motor skills. His behavior may also present a significant educational handicap." They listed his intelligence test score as 79, which in Ohio allowed the public schools to assign Sam to a Multiple Handicapped (MH) classroom with a functional curriculum.

Once a diagnostic label is assigned, the label follows a student around in both regular and special education classes. The yearly Individual Educational Plan (I.E.P.) designed by and for the student–with consultation by family, teachers, and school administrators–configures the student's class schedule but doesn't usually change the "primary" disability designation. Instead, a kind of reification occurs, whereby the student becomes the diagnostic label. The label dictates how teachers and administrators respond to the student, with enormous consequences to the student's educational opportunities.

Two years later, at our and his teacher's prodding, another school psychologist tested Sam, this time acknowledging his visual and fine motor problems by using the Perkin's-Binet Intelligence Scale for the Blind. The psychologist arrived at a score of 92, which allowed Sam to be placed in a Visually Handicapped class with a regular, though adapted, academic curriculum. Since then Sam's IQ scores have ranged between 90 and 115, depending on the test used, the testing situation, and the rapport between him and the evaluator.

Sam was included in a regular classroom, with help from a Learning Disability (LD) center, from grades 2–6. But then he entered junior high, where for the first time in his education he was asked to change class every 50 minutes (along with 1,200 other students). In fact, the school was so overcrowded that the administration had created one-way hallways. To make matters worse, Sam was not provided with an aide, as his I.E.P. stipulated. The result was predictable. His behavior problems resurfaced worse than ever. That allowed school administrators to move him from the LD center to an MH unit, where he remained, with some modifications, for the remainder of his education.

During those years I attended dozens of meetings at different schools with teachers, counselors, and administrators where Sam was labeled willful, disruptive, and intransigent. Every meeting reminded me of the Center, so many years earlier. I heard the same accusations, the same negativity, over and over and over. Even more depressing, I suppose, is that every other autistic person or blogger I've encountered has had the same exact experiences with labels. In her Processing in Parts blog a young woman named Zilari writes about being constantly analyzed and classified because of her behavior. Labeled "emotionally disturbed" and "retarded," sometimes even by her mother, Zilari encountered the same relentless negativity that Sam lived with every day. "I was considered to be deliberately willful, and arrogant, and rude," she writes in one post. Not only that, but those around her sometimes felt that she would need therapy for her entire life and "might be better off in some sort of 'placement.'"

Have these people never heard of self–fulfilling prophecies?

Congress enacted the Americans with Disabilities Act (ADA) in 1990 to "establish a clear and comprehensive prohibition of discrimination on the basis on disability." The ADA, along with the Individuals with Disabilities Education Act (IDEA) and its amendments in the 1990s, mandated an end to discriminatory practices in areas such as education, housing, and employment. But exactly what the ADA and IDEA require, and how the laws should be applied, is still being negotiated in state and federal courts. Often state and federal laws disagree on disability issues. Much of state disability law is archaic, dating from the American eugenics move-ment (1910–1940) or earlier.

Eugenics, or the science of better breeding, took two distinct forms: positive eugenics, which attempted to encourage people of "good" genetic stock to reproduce; and negative eugenics, which attempted to discourage, even prevent, people of "bad" genetic stock from reproducing. Committees such as the Committee on Eugenics and the Committee to Eradicate Feeblemindedness sponsored strategies and legislation to control feeblemindedness, including institutionalization and forced sterilization. Eventually more than 30 states enacted forced sterilization laws. State law in virtually every state still constructs people with disabilities in such terms as: "physically defective," "feeble-minded," "mentally deficient," "idiot," "imbecile," "mental defective," "lunatic," and "*non compos mentis*" (not master of one's mind). Such constructions, hardly neutral or value-free, run throughout state law and can result in the legal state of "civil death."

Sam's experiences are similar to those of most disabled people. The very institutions meant to serve them often participate in the construction of the negative stereotypes and the stigma attached to disability. If you think about it, this institutional involvement isn't surprising in a culture with such entrenched hostility toward difference and diversity. After all, disability is a manifestation of difference.

Problem is, neurodiversity doesn't test. Or rather, it doesn't lend itself to be measured by standardized tests, which (as all educators know) are designed for standardized, neuro-typical people. People who score well on such tests tend to come from families who are at the high end of the socio-economic scale and who have lots of cultural capital. We knew from the beginning that Sam was neurologically different; after all, his brain was dysmorphic, or shaped differently than the typical. So it would be logical to assume that his visual-perceptual and cognitive abilities would be atypical. And it would be just as logical to assume that he wouldn't be a whiz at taking standardized tests.

Early on, Sam demonstrated alternative ways of relating to the world. For example, when Sam was a toddler he "heard" colors along with sounds until finally, after several years of being told otherwise, therapists and teachers convinced him that he was imagining the colors. Later, even his teachers had to admit that he had super-sensitive hearing, able to hear certain sounds, especially sirens and phones, before they became audible to others. Or that he had incredible recall, able to remember large amounts of factual information (weather reports, for example) and repeat the information verbatim. Many of the problems Sam encountered at school came down to the fact that what interested him did not interest others. Instead of praising his memory, teachers would often criticize his lack of focus and his inability to generalize from disparate facts.

Eventually, the failure Sam experienced at school became a heavy burden, too heavy for him to bear. He would come home literally reeking of perspiration from the tension of trying to maintain his composure. Often he would hide or destroy the notes his teachers sent home recounting his daily transgressions, his "behaviors" *du jour*. The resulting "disciplinary action" increased in frequency every year, as he would be sent to the office or suspended for a day or two, sometimes longer, for various infractions.

During Sam's high school years I remained on pins and needles from 8 A.M. to 2 P.M., waiting for the phone to ring. It was hard to concentrate on anything. I dreaded the familiar call: Come get Sam. He's in the principal's office. He hit one of his teachers. Then I'd drive down to his school, where I'd find him sitting in the office, anxious and agitated. When I brought him home, he would sit silent and sullen at the kitchen table for hours, sometimes until he fell asleep in the chair. On the very worst days he would hit me in the car on the way home; other times he would bang his head against the side window. Bang! Bang! Bang! Trying to erase the memory of his latest failure.

Other autistic people have written about experiencing this sense of failure at school, including Joel Smith, who maintains This Way of Life, an autism advocacy website. He explains in his NTs Are Weird blog: "At school, I was a failure. I didn't do very well academically except in the rare class where my executive function didn't get in my way. I did even worse socially."

Like Smith, Sam had problems with his "executive function," his ability to perform on demand for teachers, counselors, and psychologists. "Executive dysfunction involves problems with planning and executing tasks," Smith writes. This includes sometimes even the simplest tasks, such as grooming and other daily living activities. How to counter executive dysfunction? Smith doesn't have much advice for others, since people will be affected at different times and for different reasons. In addition, people possess different strengths and weaknesses, as well as differing abilities to cope. There is no single sure-fire antidote to executive dysfunction that all autistic people can use all of the time.

Likewise, Donna Williams in *Nobody Nowhere: The Extraordinary Autobiography of an Autistic*, admits that she "could neither apply myself at school nor be told what to do." Her behaviors, as well as her coping mechanisms, continually got her in trouble: "I would talk and talk, regardless of whether any of my classmates was listening or not. The teacher would get louder, and so would I. She would send me to stand outside the classroom. I would go for a walk. She would tell me to stand in the corner. I would spit and shout: 'No!' She would try to come near me. I would arm myself with a chair like some sort of wild animal. She would shout. I would bring the chair crashing down or throw it across the room."

Sam's way of coping with executive dysfunction? He, too, acted out to divert attention from his inability to perform, his inability to execute whatever command or battery of tests he was given and expected to complete. He became the master of disorder, the disorganizer. Instead of arranging, he would disarrange. If they wanted him to match, he would jumble. During his last IQ test, administered by a high school psychologist, he started banging on a computer keyboard until the barrage of questions stopped. For years he had been treated like a circus performer expected to jump through hoops on command, but no more. Enough hoops!

Sam also resented being constantly asked how he felt. "Are you feeling okay today, Sam?" people at school would ask. "Are you doing okay?"

Of course, what they were really asking was if he had his behaviors under control, whether he would cooperate that day.

All that explains, more or less, why Sam's very first evaluator back at the Center for Developmental Disorders declared him untestable and kicked him out. Here's the scoop. We arrived early at the Center, wanting to make a good impression. Sam looked his dapper best, dressed for success in brightly colored overalls and chattering nonstop to anyone who cared to chatter back. Happy to be out and about, he toddled around the waiting room, which was packed with other parents and children who'd made the same mistake we had by arriving early. "Indubitably!" he told everyone he approached.

"Indubitably" can be cute, coming from a bushy 5-year-old with lots of attitude. But a funny thing happens after about an hour. Cute kids don't seem so cute, especially one now crawling and jumping around the room yelling, "Indubitably!" Like any kid after an hour in a packed waiting room, Sam had gone from happy to restless to OFF THE WALL.

Finally, 90 minutes late, our evaluator arrived. She took us down the hall to a testing room, my wife and I practically dragging Sam behind us. Our evaluator didn't bother to apologize for being late; instead, she started complaining about car problems, which had delayed her. As if we cared about her car problems. We wanted to get the test over ASAP and get Sam out of there fast, before he totally deconstructed. They had no idea!

Frazzled, she began organizing her testing materials. When she accidentally spilled a container of blocks on the floor, she cursed and bent over to pick up the blocks. But when she handed them to Sam and asked him to fit them together in a particular way, he purposely spilled the blocks on the floor (mimicking her), then clapped his hand and howled with laughter.

That was it! We were history, out of there, tossed faster than Lou Piniella after kicking first base into right field. "Untestable!" the evaluator said.

"Indubitably!" replied Sam.

Lucky us, the evaluator didn't give up totally. Instead, she began visiting Sam's nearby preschool until she'd spent enough time with him to claim she eventually finished the evaluation. So that the Center could send us a bill.

When we received the official report, we fired off an angry letter, pointing out the absurdity of using a standard Stanford-Binet intelligence test on a 5-year-old with Sam's problems and the irregularities of the testing situation, including the irate evaluator and the incident of the spilled blocks.

Their response began as follows: "We are sorry that the CDD evaluation of Sam was such a stressful and unsatisfactory experience for you and your family. We're sure it is difficult enough to have a child with multiple medical and educational needs, without the added stress...."

In other words, the problem was ours. They ignored the substance of our complaints and dismissed us as emotionally distraught, stressed-out parents.

Indubitably!

Chapter 4

Why Is He Barking?

We're waiting in line at the local McDonald's with what appears to be our entire neighborhood. Everyone's hungry, everyone's grumpy. But no one's quite as hungry and grumpy as Sam, who has no patience for anything, especially waiting for food. To make matters worse, the crowd and the noise level make him nervous. He squeezes my hand tightly, and then pinches me, trying to relieve the tension. Today nothing seems to help his anxiety.

"WOOOF!" Sam roars.

"I bet your pardon?" the woman in front of us asks.

I blurt out something inane like, "Oh, that's my son, Sam ... he barks."

"WOOOF!" Sam barks again, as if on command.

Maybe I should tell him to roll over and play dead.

"Listen, Sam," I say in a desperate attempt to prevent an embarrassing public meltdown. "If you don't want to wait, we can leave. It's up to you."

Put like that, Sam reconsiders his options. He reaches out and gently takes the woman's hand, holding on to it like he would a lifesaver. He attempts to strike up a conversation, another coping mechanism. "What do think of all this new construction?" Sam asks. "What do you think of all these people moving to West Chester? Do you think we can do anything about it?"

The woman laughs nervously. "Well, that's a good question. I don't know how you stop development."

"Do you have any kids?" Sam asks, on to another subject.

By the time she's finished answering that question, she finds herself next in line at the counter. "You go ahead," she says to Sam, who doesn't mind if he does.

"Hi Sam," says Ashley, our cashier, a young woman who's friendly with Sam.

"Hi Ashley. Have you been in trouble today?" Just the day before we'd heard the manager yell at Ashley for some unspecified infraction. We still don't know why. Sam likes to think it was for something egregious.

"No way," she says, entering his order on the electronic keyboard without asking him what he wants. Medium fry, medium Coke. The same thing he always orders for his mid-afternoon snack.

Most restaurants in our community welcome Sam with open arms. For many of them, he's their best customer. He might not be a big spender, but he's certainly their most regular and loyal patron. The servers know him, and they know exactly what he will order, since his order never changes. The friendliest of the servers will come over to Sam's table, sit down next to him, and talk awhile. Even some of the managers will visit with Sam. They'll shoot the breeze about the weather or the local news. Sam reads the local and national pages of our newspaper, though his favorite remains the weather page. In fact, he subscribes to *USA Today* just because he admires all the bright colors on the weather page.

Sam tends to be more able and willing to control his "behaviors" in public than in private, where he feels less restrained. But I'll still hear the occasional "WOOOF!" if he gets nervous when we're out and about.

Other behaviors are more nuanced.

For example, when Sam wants attention he might start tapping loudly on walls or tabletops. Or he might upend a piece of furniture or start flipping a light switch on and off. But these same behaviors can mean something else entirely, depending on his mood and the situation. If there's any tension in the room, between his parents or even his two older sisters when they come to visit, Sam will tap or flip or whatever, just to disrupt the emotional discord. According to the official line, Sam as an autistic person should not be adept at reading social codes and situations. Yet Sam has an extraordinarily acute emotional antenna, able to detect even the slightest hint of an argument or a disagreement. This puts additional stress on my wife and I, because when we disagree, we have to keep it on the down-low. Hard to have a really good, healthy argument in silence!

Rocking, another of Sam's behaviors, has caused him a good deal of grief over the years. Especially when he was younger, Sam would rock his head from side to side as a way to comfort himself, or sometimes as a way of focusing his attention (say, on a homework assignment). Lots of autistic people rock; it's a common behavior. In *Nobody Nowhere: The Extraordinary Autobiography of an Autistic*, Donna Williams explains her reasons for rocking: to "Provide security and release, and thereby decrease, built-up inner anxiety and tension, thereby decreasing fear. The more extreme the movement, the greater the feeling I was trying to combat."

No big deal. Or so we thought. But Sam's rocking suddenly became a big deal when he entered junior high and encountered hard-assed, disciplinary teachers who objected to the behavior, which they considered disruptive and inappropriate. They decided to take it upon themselves to eliminate Sam's behavior by, at times, holding him down physically. The inevitable happened, of course. Fisticuffs ensued, with one teacher claiming to have been pushed or struck (the incident report wasn't clear on this). As a result of the incident, Sam was reassigned to a low-level Multiple Handicap class and the teachers were taken off Sam's case.

Generally, though, these benign behaviors don't pose a problem. At least for those of use who know Sam. Strangers sometimes have a different reaction, but so what? That's their problem. Woofing, rocking, and tapping just happen to be a part of Sam's personality, who he is. Why do we all have to look and behave the same? If you think about it, lots of people have irritating habits and behaviors. How many times have you been trapped in an elevator with, or seated next to, a loudmouth with a cell phone who won't shut up, who wants to make every seamy detail of his/her private life public? Or how about the sports louts at the bar, slapping and shoving and hollering for their favorite teams? Surely, these indiscretions are more annoying than a little "WOOOF!" or a little head rocking. And you know what? I've never once seen anyone go up to a cell phone loud-mouth or a sports lout and tell them to "SHUT UP!" Or worse, try to wrestle away their cell phone or hold them down physically!

So why are annoying behaviors committed by neuro-typicals considered "normal" and therefore okay, while annoying behaviors committed by atypicals considered not normal, something to be corrected or extinguished? Kassiane Montana takes on this issue in her Rett Devil blog (she has Rett's Disorder). "What on earth is a 'behavior'?" she asks. "Normal" people don't seem to have them, only folks with developmental disabilities. "Eating, breathing, going to the bathroom, expressing needs and wants ... are all 'behaviors.' But when talking about people with developmental disabilities, the word seems to mean something different." She continues: "A behavior is something negative that someone with a disability does that needs extinguished? Is that the new definition?"

Normative pressure can be overwhelming. Neuro-typicals (I include myself) have no idea. We simply don't understand how powerful and destructive this pressure can be. The autistic blogger Elmindreda likens this forced normalization to "emotional abuse" and writes about the "damage" it can do to those who must hide or change their natural behaviors: "Being forced to hide my natural behaviour [sic] and refrain from using functional coping strategies, for no reason but the comfort of bigots, made me *far* more disabled than my autism ever has."

Elmindreda explains that her parents tried their best to teach her not to "stim" (to engage in self-stimulating behaviors). Even though she was taught that stimming was "wrong" and "bad," she did it anyway because it was a need and not a bad habit or atten-tion-getting device. However, the parental damage had been done. Because she was made to feel terrible about her self-stimulating behaviors, stimming became far less effective for relieving stress.

When parents and teachers fail to understand these needs, bad things happen. In a sense it's a failure of communication. Neuro-typicals can't "read" self-stimulating behaviors, so the autistic person gets more and more frustrated until meltdown occurs. Then, when the person becomes aggressive or self-destructive, this is the behavior that gets noticed and commented on, which reinforces the stress, and so on. It's a vicious circle.

I don't disagree with the autistic bloggers here. No doubt about it, parents and teachers misreading or ignoring autistic communications can cause meltdown. So it becomes absolutely essential for these neuro-typicals to pay attention to what autistic people say and do, since body movements and behaviors are as much a language as words.

But sometimes with Sam it's more complicated than miscommunication. Sam can always express himself, but sometimes he gets confused and can't make even a simple decision. It's as though his mind gets caught in a loop. He's conflicted. He can't decide whether to stay in or go out to a movie. Whether to go to Pizza Hut or Wendy's for lunch. Unless he can somehow get himself out of the loop, confusion will turn into agitation. Then he wants to hurt someone. Either himself or whomever he happens to be with.

As much time as I spend "listening" to Sam, sometimes his confusion, his internal pressure will build to the point where he needs to bang his head against the wall for release. From the outside, it seems as though he needs the electronic discharge that comes from smashing his head against the wall. Call it a neurological reboot, a jump start. Afterwards, he's usually calm and contrite, worrying about how he looks and if he hurt anyone else.

After one recent incident, my wife asked Sam why he'd banged his head. His response: "Because I didn't want to hurt dad."

And for the most part he doesn't hurt other people. Anymore. This has been the most important change in Sam's life over the last few years, because it's allowed him to live semi-independently. He had to learn not to hurt other people. That's pretty much the bottom line for being allowed to run free. For everyone. Sam has

learned the hard way that if he hurts other people, he gets sent to
the hospital psych ward. Or worse.

Savvy and observant, Sam knows about the institution in
Columbus. He's been warned by Emergency Room doctors and
psychiatrists. His former neurologist told him, point-blank, that if
he couldn't control his aggressive behaviors, he would have to go live
in an institution.

A cruel message, but one that Sam seems to have internalized.
He knows that violence can't be tolerated. Barking might be overlooked, but not hitting. He's worked hard to control his aggressive
impulses, which were present even when he was a toddler. But at
puberty, with his hormones raging, the aggressive behaviors
exploded. He began lashing out at people, hitting and scratching
faces. Several times at school he grabbed and tried to choke his aide.
He couldn't keep his hands to himself. He was kicked out of work
study programs as well as summer camps. After he graduated from
high school with an equivalent degree, he was kicked out of both
vocational school and sheltered workshop.

Things were equally bad at home. Sam would hover over his
boombox, blasting his music louder and louder until he worked
himself into a frenzy. Then he would go on a rampage through the
house, attacking whoever tried to turn the music down. At about the
age of 18, Sam reached rock bottom. I feared we might lose him. In
fact, I had to call 911 and ask for help on three different occasions.
Each time Sam ended up being taken to a hospital psych ward. Like
Sam, I felt defeated. I felt as though I had failed him. The two of us
together couldn't seem to make his life work.

Painful memories. And yet it was on the psych ward that Sam
began his long climb back. By talking to ward staff, he began to
internalize what so many people had told him over the years.
Medication also helped. He'd been on an anti-seizure drug since
having two seizures at the age of 12. When the ward psychiatrists
added a mood stabilizer and a new anti-psychotic, the combination
of meds helped him turn the corner.

Most autistic bloggers campaign against the evils of medication, but I can't join the crusade. Without his meds, I don't know where Sam would be today.

Sam deserves most of the credit, though. It takes an enormous effort for him to resist the impulse to grab or hit. Sometimes today he'll hold his hands behind his back when he talks to people, as a way of reminding himself to control his impulses. Restraining himself voluntarily. Avoiding what he knows will happen if he loses all control.

For my part, I've learned to pay attention to what Sam wants, not to what others want for him. Early on, I signed him up for various programs and sent him to lots of summer camps. While he enjoyed these outings when he was in grade school, he resented them once he hit puberty. My eyes were opened one Monday morning. Sam and I were on a 200-mile drive to the best special needs camp in the state, when suddenly Sam started opening the car door and twisting the rear view mirror. It was a horrifying experience. I must have pulled over on the shoulder of the highway a half dozen times before we arrived at camp. I didn't know what to do. Sam was telling me by his actions that he no longer wanted to attend camp. But we had driven so far, we had spent so much money on the week-long stay. Rationalizations, I know. And in the end I did the wrong thing: I left Sam there. Two days later I had to come get him, after several incidents with camp staff.

The same thing happened at the vocational school that Sam attended after high school. His high school teachers thought Sam might do well in an office training program at the school. I bit my tongue. But always the dutiful companion, I drove Sam to school and picked him up for the first three days. On day four, about an hour after I dropped him off, my phone rang. Come pick up Sam, he's banging on his desk and screaming obscenities. Fuck! Fuck! Fuck! I got the picture. No more vocational school for Sam.

My bad again when, pressured by the county Mental Retardation and Developmental Disabilities agency, I agreed to send Sam to a sheltered workshop. MRDD wanted to make sure Sam had work opportunities. Oh boy, did he ever. For 24 cents an hour they expected Sam to sit still long enough to sort screws one at a time, then place them in appropriate boxes. Sheltered workshops serve a purpose (I guess), but the thing about them is that they're designed for a particular kind of client: a slow moving, rather passive client who can sit still for long periods of time. Well, sorry, but Sam can't sit still for even short periods of time. He's a high-octane kind of guy who races through life. Adding insult to injury, Sam still lacks the depth perception and fine motor skills necessary to sort screws. In other words, the well-intentioned folks at the workshop could not have found a more inappropriate job to assign Sam.

You can guess what happened. Every day Sam rebelled after about five minutes of sorting screws, raised hell, and was tossed out. Pretty quickly his "work opportunity" evolved into a babysitting session Monday and Wednesday mornings, where one of the coaches would sit with Sam and talk about the weather. For two hours. But Sam hated the workshop so much that not even weather talk could make the experience tolerable. Even MRDD had to agree with me that the workshop wasn't for Sam when he grabbed one of the aides from his former high school (there helping another client) and placed the poor unsuspecting woman in a chokehold.

Since the workshop disaster Sam has made his own decisions about what he wants to do and where he wants to go. "Butt out!" he'll say, if I or anyone else starts suggesting where we shouldn't be suggesting. Sometimes I wish he'd be more active in the community, but I keep my mouth shut. Sam does what he does, nothing more, nothing less. His repertoire includes rap music, food, movies, and weather. Forget work. He's the Family Gangsta!

Years later, when I read an essay by Sue Rubin, I understood a bit more about why Sam loathed the workshop so much. In her short essay, "Killing Autism Is a Constant Battle," Rubin writes about trying to avoid other autistic people "because they make me more autistic." That is, because seeing them (and their behaviors) makes it more difficult for her to control her behaviors. Like Rubin, Sam tries to avoid other autistic people because they can set off his behaviors (and also, I think, because he gets a glimpse of how he looks to others).

Come to think of it, he tries to avoid other disabled people in general, even though he knows and believes in disability rights. He'll often pump his fist in the air and say, "GIMPS RULE!"

I see this conflicted dynamic at work in a recent love-hate friendship Sam had with another young man with disabilities. Mike worked at the local Kroger, where he would bag groceries and badger the customers with weird talk about "rubber chickens" and other bizarre topics. For whatever reason, he took a liking to Sam. So whenever he saw Sam walk into the store, he made a beeline toward his (he thought) compatriot. "Hi Grampa!" he would shout out to Sam from across the store. Or "Hi Elvis!" "Hi Beevis!" Every time it was a different name, intended as a joke (I think).

Sam failed to see the humor. In fact, he found Mike's banter insulting, not only because it was utterly inappropriate and down-right goofy, but because it made their disabilities visible and held them both up to ridicule in PUBLIC. For everyone to see and hear. A freak show!

Their friendship (if you can call it that) deteriorated to the point that whenever Mike approached, Sam would let loose a panicked "WOOOF!" and run the other way.

Much to Sam's relief, Mike was transferred to another Kroger store last summer. Still, whenever he walks into our Kroger, Sam looks around to make sure he doesn't see his former tormentor or hear any rubber chicken talk.

Chapter 5

Sensory Overload

Sam stands, horrified, looking at the Puffer. His mother steps into the glass enclosure, the door closing behind her. Then PUFF, a blast of air shoots up from the floor and ruffles her clothing. She stands perfectly still for several long seconds while the machine analyzes the chemical traces released by the current of air. When the door on the other side opens, she steps out and motions for Sam to follow. He freezes.

We're at the airport, flying to Miami for our annual Christmas week vacation. Holiday travelers jam the terminal, from the parking garage all the way to security. At every counter there's another long line of travelers, but none as long as the line to get through security. We've stood in line for what seems like hours, with Sam getting more nervous every time we inch ahead. He's managed to make it this far, to the X-ray and Puffer machines, without a meltdown. He's grabbed, he's pinched, he's pushed, but he's kept moving forward. Until now.

"Come on, Sam," his mother says, motioning him forward.

"Go on, Sam," I say, pointing at the green light.

"DON'T touch the sides!" the security guard yells.

Then I step back a moment, realizing how Sam must feel. Everybody's yelling at him. He's overloaded, overwhelmed. I try to give him some space, but the people behind us are pushing forward, impatient.

Sam looks around, his pupils dilated. He's like a trapped animal, looking for a way to escape. Fight or flight.

For a moment I think he's about to lash out.

"It's okay, Sam," I say. "Take your time. When you're ready, just step forward. We're almost through security. This is the last thing."

Just as the security guard is about to lose patience, Sam takes a tentative step forward. "DON'T!" the guard yells again, as Sam reaches out to grab the side. The guard doesn't understand that Sam, like most visually impaired people, reaches out instinctively for something or someone to anchor him.

But Sam manages to stand still long enough for the door to close.

PUFF!

When the air shoots up, Sam flaps his hands, startled, even though he knew the blast of air was coming.

"Sam, you did it!" his mother says, as he steps out.

"Good job," the security guard says.

Still shaking, Sam puts on his shoes and backpack. He's feeling calmer now. He's going to make it. We'd promised him lunch after security, and now he's ready to collect.

Like most autistic people, Sam gets overloaded in stressful situations where people are yelling directions or demands at him. He can't process the information fast enough. So he freezes or shuts down altogether. If the yelling continues, he's liable to go off and hurt himself or someone else. The same thing happened at school, at summer camp, and at the sheltered workshop.

Sometimes it's not any one particular event that "causes" a meltdown. Rather, tension will build during a day or a week until one seemingly innocuous occurrence will trigger an explosion. This makes it more difficult to foresee or prevent a meltdown. As Joel Smith explains in his blog, NTs Are Weird: "Often, the little insults, problems, and stresses will build up over time, until the point where one ... will be just enough to make it too much to handle." He goes on to say that, unlike neuro-typicals, autistic people might not give any warning signals until it's too late. To understand the dynamics, we have to look at the whole situation, not just the last trigger. In fact, the last trigger may have been the least significant contributor to the meltdown/shutdown.

Some days Sam will wake up on the wrong side of the bed. He'll be sullen, edgy, with a faraway look in his eye. Not even his rap music will perk him up. On these days I try to help him avoid all stressful situations. I make sure to place no demands on him. Instead, I slow down. I try to move through the day in slow motion. I talk to him in a quiet, matter-of-fact voice. Chill. Be cool. That's the strategy.

Sometimes the strategy works. The quiet, steady companionship will turn around his mood. His eyes will refocus. He'll come back to the here and now. Back to being Sam.

On the bad days nothing works. It's similar to watching someone with epilepsy. You can see the seizure (or the meltdown) coming, but you can't head off what's about to happen. Get ready to duck and run for the door. That's about all you can do.

Even though I've been chased around the house more times than I care to remember, I still empathize with Sam. He's so easily overwhelmed by the demands of daily living. Just showering, dressing, preparing food, shopping, relating to the people he encounters in the course of his day, all the things neuro-typicals take in stride, can overburden him to the point of no return.

I've come to recognize — and even admire — Sam's coping strategies. He establishes his routines and then follows them exactly. Everything becomes ritualized, which is his way of bringing order to the chaos of experience. Preferring a one-on-one situation, he attaches himself to a single person and does one thing at a time. He avoids multiple tasks and group situations, for those involve too many conflicting lines of communication. Too much static.

Every day Sam struggles to balance what he needs to do with what his coping strategies will allow him to do.

Nearly all autistic bloggers comment on this same struggle. In her blog, Andrea's Buzzing About, Andrea writes about her difficulty juggling the demands of life. She uses a metaphor to illustrate the problem: the TV variety show entertainer who spins plates on top of sticks, rushing from one plate to another to re-spin them before they slow down enough to fall. "You know what happens when you have too many plates spinning; one is likely to get away from you (*crash!*) as you devote time to another," she writes. "Then there are the days when my plate-spinning skills suck. I get too overwhelmed by the quantities of novel inputs I am trying to sort out, or the numbers of simultaneous inputs that all require high-level cognitive work, combined with my internal processing glitches."

When her processing gets overloaded, she continues, "my perceptions of things around me are reduced. Objects are not individually distinct, but can erratically devolve into indistinct patterns of color and lighting. I cannot identify people by my usual gestalts of nonfacial characteristics, and sometimes I don't even perceive them as people but just as moving objects. Some kinds of visuals, such as high-contrast vertical stripes or flashing things derail my attention completely, leaving me frozen and entranced."

Like Andrea, Sam's overloads can result from both internal dissonance as well as external causes (such as crowds and loud noises). Though visually impaired, Sam has hypersensitive hearing and touch. Sirens, for example, will almost always set him off. He freezes the instant he hears a siren. He'll cover his ears with both hands until it stops. When he was a toddler, we would take him to parades and festivals that sometimes included emergency vehicles. Just the sight of a fire truck would prompt him to cover his ears. As he got older, as a way of desensitizing himself, he would ask to sit in the front seat of a parked fire truck. Firefighters would usually accommodate Sam, hoisting him up into the driver's seat. But instead of grabbing the steering wheel, Sam would grab his ears!

Sirens and other high-pitched sounds tend to be the worst, but even lower sounds like people talking and dogs barking (for example) can set Sam off if he's on edge. Hearing the telephone ring can also trigger a meltdown. Other autistic people share this hypersensitivity to sound. Temple Grandin explains her sensitivity in "An Insider's View of Autism." Grandin writes: "My hearing is like having a hearing aid with the volume control stuck on 'super loud.' It is like an open microphone that picks up everything. I have two choices: turn the mike on and get deluged with sound, or shut it off. I am unable to talk on the phone in a noisy office or airport. Everybody else can use the phones in a noisy environment, but I can't. If I try to screen out the background noise, I also screen out the phone."

We do what we can to address Sam's hypersensitivity to sound. We can't eliminate sirens or stop emergency vehicles from operating in our neighborhood. But we can do the small things. We turn down the ringer on our phone. We wait until he's out of the house before we vacuum or use any appliance or machine that makes a lot of noise. Our house has become a Quiet Zone.

Not surprisingly, Sam also has tactile issues. I say not surprisingly because sensitivity to touch is common among people with autism. His reaction to being touched depends on his mood. One day he'll be high-fiving and jostling with me or the other guys he hangs with, and the next he'll cringe at the slightest touch. When he's in this mood, he's been known to swat or head-butt as a means to keep people "outta my face," as he says.

Touching others can also be a problem for Sam. Unable to gauge tactile pressure, he's not aware of how tightly he's holding or grabbing someone. Sometimes he thinks he's being affectionate when he's actually strangling the hapless object of his affection. His squeeze resembles a vise grip. This inability to modulate pressure has made it hard for Sam to have friends or to find what he calls a "C" (for companion). The ladies tend to shy away from Sam after he grabs them once or twice. Strangleholds will do that. Guys are more tolerant, but their tolerance wears thin after a certain number of scratches and bruises.

Temple Grandin has written extensively about tactile issues in autism. In addition to her role as spokesperson for Asperger's and her work in animal science, Grandin is famous for designing a "hug" machine. Once she crawls inside the machine, a control panel allows her to regulate the pressure and duration of her "hugs." Prior to creating the machine, Grandin had a deep aversion to being hugged. In "My Experiences with Visual Thinking, Sensory Problems, and

Communication Difficulties" Grandin explains her aversion: "I pulled away when people tried to hug me, because being touched sent an overwhelming tidal wave of stimulation through my body. I wanted to feel the comforting feeling of being held, but then when somebody held me, the effect on my nervous system was overwhelming. It was an approach-avoid situation, but sensory over stimulation caused the avoidance."

To treat tactile hypersensitivity, Grandin recommends strategies such as deep pressure stimulation and gently stroking an autistic child with different cloth textures.

Early on, Sam had lots of physical therapy, including deep pressure stimulation and massage. That all changed when Sam entered his teens. Now no one dares touch him without his permission. The last person who tried to move in uninvited got a punch in the nose. We still give him hugs and massage his shoulders, but only when he initiates the physical contact. Sam has to make the first move. Otherwise, we keep our distance, thank you.

Sam met his match at the sheltered workshop he attended briefly. Her name was Chrissy, a young woman about Sam's age who was a real live hugging machine. Chrissy didn't talk, but she was a connoisseur of deep hugs. She took an immediate liking to Sam and would literally chase him around the workshop until she had him cornered. Then she'd move in for the hug — a long, deep, crushing, no-holds-barred bear hug!

Shocked that someone would grab as hard as he did, Sam didn't know how to react. Should he smack her? Should he hug her back? What?

At first he tried to escape, but then he decided he sort of liked the hugs. "Chrissy likes me," he would brag.

And she did. Sam was Chrissy's number one squeeze, probably because he gave as good as he got.

Ironically for someone known as the master of chaos, Sam goes bonkers whenever his routine is disrupted. Sam thinks nothing of disrupting other people, especially when he's asked to do something. He'll spit out his meds and pour his glass of water on the counter, he'll drop a tray of cookies on the floor, he'll knock over a lamp or a stack of CDs.

But if his own daily routine isn't EXACTLY the same every day, he gets overloaded with worry, anxiety, or whatever. Shower, lunch, dinner, everything must be tightly scripted. No room for spontaneity. He has to walk at the same time and place, he has to go to the same movie theater, the same Kroger store. Everything has to be predictable.

If something goes wrong, watch out! Say if one of his other companions can't come as scheduled that day, I keep my distance and stay light on my feet.

Sam doesn't understand that some things can't be controlled. An appliance stops working, an electronic device breaks, the cable goes out, all the little mishaps and annoyances that occur on a regular basis. For most of us, we deal with the problem. We call the repair person or the cable company. No biggie.

Not so for Sam, who can't tolerate any chaos around him (except what he creates himself!). This makes it difficult when we have to call plumbers and electricians to make noisy repairs at our house. It's even worse when repairs have to be made in his pad, the Yellow Submarine. The idea that things break down is deeply disturbing to Sam, almost a phobia. Not only do broken things disrupt his routine, they feed his anxiety.

The need for stability extends to Sam's obsession with the weather. As much as he talks about severe weather, he comes unglued whenever the National Weather Service issues a severe weather watch, especially a tornado watch. From the outside, it's as though he's neurologically affected by the change in pressure. He'll pace the house like a caged animal. He'll listen to the radio for a few seconds and then watch the Weather Channel for a few seconds. When he's tired of watching TV, he'll head for his computer and check the online weather sites he's bookmarked.

If rain develops on the way to a movie theater or restaurant, Sam will often refuse to get out of the car. On stormy days, forget about it.

One Father's Day a few years ago we took Sam to a Cincinnati Reds baseball game. The ballpark was packed, but we managed to talk Sam through the noise and the crowd. Unfortunately, once we were seated, the unpredictable happened: a light rain began to fall. We took shelter under the roof of a nearby concession stand, intending to wait for the rain to stop. But Sam freaked. He couldn't deal with the rain (in addition to the mass of noisy people trying to find shelter). He insisted we leave, pushing and shoving to get our attention. When I tried to convince him to stay, he reared back and punched me in the face.

"NO!" he screamed.

So, suffering the ignominy of being punched by my son on Father's Day, I headed for the exit.

Having learned our lesson, we don't take Sam anywhere on rainy days, unless he absolutely insists on going somewhere (say, a restaurant). He stays at home and enjoys the show from the safety of his own house.

We can't stop the rain, but we try to help Sam cope with chaotic situations at home. We built the Yellow Submarine just so Sam would have his own quiet retreat — a safe, secure place to regroup on noisy or otherwise stressful days. Of course, we also wanted to increase his independence by providing him with his own fully equipped apartment, including a private entrance. His bachelor pad, he calls it. He's very particular about who he allows to enter. He'll ask what you want before giving you permission to enter.

The Yellow Submarine provides Sam with a much-needed place of refuge. He goes downstairs to escape the troubled world of problems and confusion. For Sam, learning to do this has been a major accomplishment because he's learned to manage himself. In a tense situation, instead of hanging around and getting overloaded, he'll take control by walking away. On occasion, even though we beg him to distance himself from the stressor, he'll stick it out to the bitter end and the inevitable will happen. But most of the time he goes down to his pad.

The Yellow Submarine also comes in handy when Sam's

nephews come to visit. Hyperactive rug rats, both Calvin and Jessie are as perpetual motion as Sam. On Calvin's most recent visit, he raced around the house getting in to one thing after another, his mother chasing along behind. Total mayhem.

Sam was patient for a good many days. One day, though, he'd finally had enough. He shook his head and said, "This place is a mad house!" Then he headed for the safety of the Yellow Submarine.

His sister laughed. "You're a fine one to talk!"

Chapter 6

Meltdown

We'd spent the evening in the Emergency Room. Sometime during the middle of the night a nurse had taken us up to a private room where Sam could stay until morning. Sam crawled into bed fully dressed. I collapsed in a nearby chair, too tired to even remove my shoes. Every hour or so a nurse would come into the room to check Sam's vital signs, further interrupting our fitful sleep.

The nightmare had begun the day before when Sam, an 18-year-old high school senior, had lost control of his behavior. He started banging his head on the wall harder than we had ever seen him, trying to do serious damage. When we tried to stop him from hurting himself, he attacked us, biting and hitting. He couldn't stop. Out of options, we called 911 and asked for help.

Sam struggled with the deputies when they arrived. But by the time they loaded him into the police cruiser, he had calmed down. He chatted about the weather as though nothing out of the ordinary had happened. Had they ever seen a tornado? Did they like sirens?

Cindy and I cleaned our wounds and then followed the police car to Children's Hospital, where we spent the longest night ever waiting for a bed to open on the Adolescent Psych Ward. It never did. So when Sam was moved upstairs to a temporary room, I went along while Cindy headed home to get some much needed sleep for whatever tomorrow would bring.

Come morning, a nurse brought Sam a breakfast tray. He picked at his food, still edgy from the night before. I could tell he was incensed that I'd made the call and had him taken to the hospital. When I tried to explain, Sam exploded. He jumped out of bed and chased me around the hospital ward until several nurses, working as a team, managed to calm him down and talk him back to his room.

I got the message. I waited outside Sam's room until the transfer occurred. Even then I kept my distance, not wanting to set him off again.

Now Sam and I sit at a conference table, across from the psychiatric nurse who's conducting the intake interview. The nurse, a tall muscular guy with a chiseled face, introduces himself as Denver and explains ward behavior rules and work schedules. He says all patients are expected to help with ward chores and to keep up with their school homework during designated timeslots, morning and afternoon. Here we go again with the old behavior mod, tough love approach.

Okay. Good luck with that, I'm thinking.

When Denver gets to visiting hours and phone privileges, Sam begins to bang his head on the top of the conference table. Not hard, but again and again, trying to drown out the litany of rules and regulations, not to mention the memory of what has happened to him over the past 24 hours.

Another nurse joins us at the table. None of us sitting in the drab institutional room mentions the blood dripping down Sam's forehead.

"Visiting hours are from 7 to 9 P.M.," Denver says. "All visitors and phone calls must be approved by the ward staff." He looks at me. "That's because families are sometimes part of the problem."

Now I'm confused. Am I part of the problem?

By this time I'm numb, overwhelmed by the supreme irony of the situation: my son is here precisely because he can't follow these rules. What do they hope to accomplish by demonstrating, once again, what he can't do?

"Do you have any questions?" asks Denver.

Sam refuses to speak. He stares straight ahead, his face pinched, sullen.

"Okay, then," Denver says, as though everything were fine and dandy.

When he asks me to leave, I panic. Leave Sam? Here? Do they know what they're doing? Have they worked with autistic teens before?

Suddenly I have a million questions I want to ask, but it's too late. Denver puts his arm around my shoulders and shuffles me toward the door. "Don't worry, he'll be fine," he says.

But will he? On the way home I feel like Judas. I keep thinking I've betrayed my son. How can I help now if they won't even let me see him?

As it turns out I needn't have worried.

When I get home, my wife greets me at the door. "You won't believe this," she says. "They want you to come back and show them how to work with Sam!"

Seeing my incredulity, she explains that one of the psychiatric aides had tried to give Sam a shower. Ward rules, no doubt. When Sam resisted, all hell broke loose in the shower. Flying soap, shampoo, and punches. No big surprise to anyone familiar with Sam. He wants prompts, not actual assistance.

So, though exhausted, it's with a certain sense of relief that I turn around and drive back down to the hospital.

Mental Status Examination
Revealed a young man with dysmorphic cranial features who was hyper-verbal, buzzing, humming, waving his hands at nurses in an aggressive manner, shaking his head and banging his head on the headboard. Patient was able to be distracted, but frequently would begin perseverative talk about singing "Happy Birthday" to policeman or buzzing like a bee. Patient was initially refusing to answer questions, and then saying no he would not answer questions. Speech noted a mild articulation problem with rapid expression. There is no evidence of clear flight of ideas, but clear distractibility and at times tangential thinking. There was no evidence of ongoing auditory or visual hallucinations currently, but this cannot be reliably ascertained. Patient denied suicidal ideation and homicidal ideation. Overall, his affect was irritable and underlying mood appeared depressed. Patient would not cooperate with cognitive at this time.
     –Samuel Wilson Admission Note, 5 October 1999

I push the buzzer and wait for the heavy metal door to snap open. For the past three days, at the request of ward staff, I've been coming down in the morning to help Sam with his shower. I come back in the afternoon for a short time and then again in the evening for visiting hours. I'm still talking with the nurses and aides about the most effective protocol for Sam. Their initial diagnosis: Hydrocephalus, Autism Spectrum Disorder, and Mood Disorder (possibly Bipolar, though there is some disagreement on the severity).

Sam is already out of bed when I walk into his room. He sits in a small metal chair staring at the door. His face is like stone. No expression, just the flat affect that means he's depressed, tense, and ready to go off. Not good.

"Hi Sam, I brought you the newspaper," I say, hoping that *USA Today*'s weather page will perk him up.

"Where were you?" he asks.

"I got here as soon as I could. It's a long drive in the morning traffic."

He lets me hand him the newspaper, glances at the weather page, and then tosses it on the bedside table. He continues to glare at me and anyone else who comes into the room.

After his shower, I help Sam get dressed. His hands are unsteady; he requires lots of prompts, lots of patience. As obsessive as ever, he puts on his clothes in the same order. He keeps his shoes beside the bed, his watch on the bed stand. Everything has to be in its place. Every act becomes a ritual. Sam can't tolerate any change in his routine.

We spend the morning reading *USA Today*. I try to be upbeat, to make conversation, but Sam does not respond. He's too far away, lost in his depression and the numbing effects of the emergency doses of Haldol they've given him. I can't get him back. My usual banter about the weather, my jokes about hospital food, nothing brings him back to the surface of the present moment, the here and now, the two of us sitting in this shabby hospital room, father and son. Not even the radio station he enjoys listening to every morning interests him. Turn it on, turn it off, he doesn't care.

Just a few minutes later the new patient who was admitted last night, who's name is Harold, begins prowling the hallway shouting and pounding on doors. Harold's pissed at someone or something; he wants to raise hell and talk to whoever's in charge here!

"Where's my damn doctor!" Harold shouts.

I see Sam's face turn white with tension. He looks terrified.

Finally he snaps. I watch, horrified, as he begins to smash his head backward against the wall behind him. When one of the nurses rushes into the room with emergency meds, Sam goes for her face, his arms flailing like windmills.

"Don't hurt her, Sam," I say, trying to help fend him off.

"Hey Sam, what's the problem?" I hear someone ask behind me. It's Denver, the psychiatric nurse who'd admitted Sam. He's tall and athletic, built like a tight end. He grabs Sam from behind, forces him to sit in a chair out in the hallway.

Denver tries to soothe Sam, telling him to calm down. "Come on, you can do it, buddy. Let's talk."

But Sam keeps struggling and screaming, "Fuck you!"

Denver has no choice. He and the other nurse maneuver Sam down the hall to the Quiet Room. I hear Sam scream as they put him in restraints, his arms and legs. They can't allow him to hurt himself or anyone else. I understand. And yet I can't bear to hear my son scream in pain. My heart is pounding; my head aches. I feel like smashing my head against the wall, too.

And then, thankfully, the screaming stops. An eerie silence comes over the ward. I stand by myself in the hallway, not knowing where to go, what to do. Then I hear Sam:

"Hey — where are my shoes?"

And again:

"Hey — where's my watch?"

"They're right here, Sam," Denver says. "You can have them as soon as you calm down."

"Okay," Sam says, quietly.

I'm tempted to laugh, even though I know how inappropriate that would be under the circumstances. Nervous tension, I suppose.

The thing is, Sam's obsessive about his shoes and his watch. He has to be able to locate them at all times. They serve as his compass; they tell him where he is in the world.

Now I hear Sam and Denver chatting softly about something.

Eventually Jenny, the other nurse, comes out of the Quiet Room and joins me. "Denver will stay with him — he's really good at this," she says. "Don't worry, we won't let Sam hurt himself."

I thank her. We talk for a while about Sam's new meds. The ward psychiatrists are changing Sam's medication. Something will help, Jenny says. We just have to find the right medication.

Left alone, I wander into the Day Room, where a number of the teenagers on the ward are doing their homework. Two of the girls, thin as rails, have feeding tubes in their noses. One of the boys has white bandages wrapped around both wrists. The three of them have been here for several weeks.

"Is Sam okay?" one of the girls asks.

Good question. "I think so." I'm trying to be as upbeat as Jenny and Denver seem to be.

That evening, when I return for visiting hours, I find Sam laughing and joking with Denver in the Day Room. They've become fast friends. Denver is helping Sam fill out his breakfast menu, crossing out the breakfast items that Sam doesn't like and writing "X 2!" for those he likes: pancakes, bacon, J-ello, and orange juice. "X 2" meaning, of course, a double serving.

"Let me show you what Denver did," Sam says. He takes me back to his room, where Denver has moved a portable TV and VCR unit off to the side of Sam's bed.

"Look," Sam says, pointing to a stack of videos on the cart. "Denver hooked me up to some movies." Ignoring me, he starts to dig through the stack of videos. I notice that he's wearing his shoes and his watch. All's right with the world once again.

So the rest of the week Sam watches movies while the other teens on the ward do their homework. Not a bad job if you can get it. Actually, Sam hasn't had any homework all year. His teachers have stopped giving him assignments. At this point they're just trying to get him through the year, so he can graduate with his class and come away with an equivalent degree. Everyone agrees that for Sam homework is meaningless.

At the end of the week Sam is discharged. His new medications have stabilized his moods enough so that he can better control his behaviors. Since the incident that landed him in the Quiet Room, he hasn't lashed out at anyone on the ward. His forehead has almost healed. He's started to relax. We're beginning to get a glimpse of the old Sam underneath the anxiety.

After a meeting with the ward psychiatrist, and another with the support staff, Sam gets his official walking papers. We go back to his room and pack his suitcase: a few clothes along with the usual collection of weather almanacs. He wants to say goodbye to the nurses, especially Denver, who's become his best friend on the ward.

He's managed to engage Denver in a never-ending weather conversation, focused specifically on the state of Kentucky, where Denver lives. Sam also likes to joke that Denver is from Denver, Colorado.

"He feels bad about putting me in the Quiet Room," Sam says before we leave. He gives us his most sincere look before adding: "He didn't have any choice, though. I understand."

We stop at the nurses station to say goodbye. Sam shakes hands and gives high fives all around. "Hey Denver, will you miss me?" he asks.

"Sure will," Denver says. "Be cool now."

"Yeah, maybe I'll come back to visit you."

"Okay...."

But Sam has already moved on. One of the other male nurses, the one Sam had wrestled with in the shower, stands guard at the door. He sees Sam coming and steps back out of the way, but Sam will have none of that. He walks right up to the guy and throws his arms around his neck. Everyone tenses, expecting the worst. Except Sam, who proceeds to give the surprised nurse a big wet kiss directly on the cheek.

Smack. The sound echoes in the hallway.

We all laugh uneasily as Sam steps through the door and heads directly for the elevator.

"Let's stop at McDonald's on the way home," Sam says. "I bet Ashley and Lisa are working today. Do I have to tell them I was on the lock-down ward?"

Chapter 7

Friends and Lovers

Every morning when Sam wakes up he's greeted by a smiling Will Ferrell and a demonic looking Mike Meyers. His roommates, as he calls them, are life-size cardboard cutouts of Will Ferrell (as Elf) and Mike Meyers (as Dr. Evil). He's partied them up a bit, hanging strands of Mardi Gras beads on Dr. Evil and placing a red Santa Claus hat on Elf. Sam also shares the Yellow Submarine with a collection of toy animals (mostly moose), an imaginary werewolf, and a plastic figurine of Frisch's Big Boy. A motley crew, for sure.

So far Sam hasn't shown any interest in moving from cardboard cutouts to real live people. I've encouraged him to think about finding a roommate, but Sam always says, "Maybe in a year or two." That's the same response he gives when asked if he wants to find a job. "Maybe in a year or two." Always cautious, Sam prefers a one-on-one situation. Groups scare him. He's become more groupaphobic as he's gotten older. Partly it's a question of control. With a roommate, he'd have to compromise, he'd have to work things out. For Sam, working things out does not compute.

Roommates might want to use his computer or TV. Worse yet, they might touch his CDs, which he keeps neatly scattered over his kitchen counters and spilling onto the floor. Touching his CD disarray constitutes a grievous crime in the world according to Sam.

Most medical sources agree that autistic people have problems with forming and maintaining friendships. Autistic people avoid eye contact; they're rigid, self-centered, and socially maladroit, unable to read social codes. Sam certainly fits that description, and yet on occasion he'll surprise me. He'll break out of that stiff, unlikable mold and genuinely relate to people. He'll notice that someone close to him feels a bit blue and ask what he can do to help. When someone in the neighborhood asks how he's doing, he'll shake the person's hand and politely say, "Thank you for asking."

Or when I'm having a bad day at home, thinking my parenting skills suck, he'll come up and put his arm around me and say, "No, you're the world's greatest father."

Still, friendship has been difficult for Sam. During elementary school he made a grand total of two friends, not counting the sons of a colleague who were obligated to be nice to Sam. The two friends were very much alike: sweet, gentle boys with a highly developed feminine side. They accepted Sam without trying to change him, perhaps because they too were a bit "different." But even they disappeared once they entered puberty, leaving Sam friendless in junior high and feeling bad about himself.

Sam's experience matches what I find in most blogs written by autistic people. "Friends are those who tolerate having me around," writes Elmindreda in her blog. "Even when I'm allowed to participate, I know that I'm not really considered part of the group," she continues. Elmindreda says she's sometimes treated like a mascot of sorts, with her presence always contingent on the pleasure of others.

Or consider Casey's story, posted by Lori Berkowitz on her LBnuke blog: "Looking back now, I would say my elementary years were terrible, no matter what ANYBODY says. I guess I did seem odd to the other children, with my limited facial expressions and vocabulary and how I flapped my hands, waved around hair ribbons, and made strange noises." Casey says that 50 percent of the other students bullied her, while the other half ignored and neglected her.

Casey wrote this post at the age of 16. She goes on to confess that by eighth grade she had begun to have suicidal thoughts, which ended only when she convinced her parents to pull her out of school (to be home-schooled): "I started to get very depressed and angry and thought about suicide a lot. I stopped hanging out with the few friends I had and kept to myself ... and cried a lot. I had started to hurt myself such as biting or scratching myself or banging my head against the walls."

Exactly. It was at this same age, and under this same social pressure, that Sam started hurting himself. One day Sam snapped, shoving or hitting his junior high LD teacher (who'd tried to physically restrain Sam from rocking). As a result, he was kicked out of the LD center and relegated to a Multiple Handicapped classroom. But ironically, Sam's social life improved after he was placed in the MH class with other students the school considered misfits. Surrounded by teens with Down Syndrome, with spina bifida, with cerebral palsy and other disabilities, Sam blossomed. Temporarily.

For a time Sam felt comfortable with his MH classmates. Copacetic, as he would say. He invited them over for a couple of parties. He went to movies and restaurants with Melissa and Katie (still the closest thing to a "date" Sam has ever had). He played T-ball with Jorge and Melissa. To this day he's still casual buds with Jorge and Katie and the lovely Nicole, who uses a wheelchair and works at the local cinema.

But Sam regards sweet Melissa as his best friend. He still calls her every day to ask how she's doing. Even if he has nothing new to report, Sam will call and ask the usual weather questions, followed by questions about her family and her job working at Wendy's. "Melissa," he'll say, "I want you to know that I'll always be there for you. You can always count on me."

Problem is, their former budding romance has become a phone relationship. So what happened?

Sexuality happened, primarily. Sam couldn't get a handle on his raging hormones. He would ask Melissa to a movie. On the way he would gently hold her hand and tell her how lovely she looked. Then in the darkened theater, during the showing of the movie, he would move in for a smooch. Never known for having a light touch, Sam would grab Melissa around the neck and forcibly kiss her. On one occasion he grabbed her in a full-body embrace. When asked to stop, Cassanova stood up and started shoving and yelling.

Other factors contributed to their stagnant relationship. They went to different high schools, for example. And when Sam ended up on an adolescent psych ward during his senior year, that experience had a profound impact on him. Since then he's been increasingly cautious about relationships. Primarily, though, I think it was the sexuality. Sam hadn't found a way to express his sexuality. He still hasn't. From the outside, it appears as though he's confused, conflicted by competing urges. Often his sexuality gets redirected to tension or repressed altogether. So far he hasn't been ready to own it. Or even talk about it.

Other similar incidents occurred during Sam's troubled and unhappy high school years. On one occasion he got fresh with a counselor while they were *en route* to McDonald's for lunch. She managed to stop the car and get out, but Sam (in an attempt to punish himself) banged his head on the door and had to be taken to the nearest hospital Emergency Room. He was apologetic in the Emergency Room, still trying to sweet talk his counselor, even though he was covered in blood.

In an attempt to help Sam deal with his sexuality, we signed him up for a sexuality workshop at the county MRDD. Little did we know that the other clients would be in their 30s, 40s, and 50s. Even some couples enrolled. Sam was totally out of his league, experientially. And when the workshop leader started talking about safe sex and intercourse, Sam freaked. He bounced up and down in his chair for the duration of the meeting. After two such meetings, the workshop leader asked us not to bring Sam back because his bouncing was disrupting the class. Seems it was hard to have a frank discussion about sex in the presence of a laughing teenager bouncing on his chair as though it were a trampoline.

Terrible years. A wasteland. The only reason Sam made it through high school was the attention of one teacher who became Sam's mentor and later his friend. Dubbed "Mr. Nickelpie" by Sam and Jorge, this very special teacher taught Sam how to cook a mean grilled cheese sandwich and a tasty hot dog. He came to know Sam as well as anyone ever has, spending hours in one-on-one discussions with Sam, always an eye-opening experience. Not that it was always perfectly platonic. Hardly. Mr. Nickelpie took his share of blows from Sam on the bad days.

Mr. Nickelpie advocated the Gentle Teaching method, the opposite of tough love. He listened, and Sam confided in him as though he were a best friend. When Sam graduated and attempted to transition to vocational school, Mr. Nickelpie wrote a letter on Sam's behalf. To this day the letter occupies a place of honor in Sam's scrapbook. It reads in part:

"One thing I find most striking about Sam is his huge vocabulary. Sam was the first, and probably the only student I will ever have, who increased my vocabulary. When I had Sam as a student I kept a dictionary handy, and often found myself looking up words he was using. He had this uncanny ability to articulate complex ideas and ask deep probing questions of just about anything you can think of, from 'how fast is the speed of light?' to 'who was your second grade teacher?' It's a little scary to think about, but in some ways Sam probably knows more about me than my wife does. I remember this most amazing conversation we had that went on for several months about the nature of time, the speed of light, and the theory of relativity among other things. He had my head throbbing thinking about subjects I had never given much thought to before. I would go home at night and research his questions."

His friendship with Mr. Nickelpie kept Sam afloat through troubled times. Years when he couldn't find a friend; when he couldn't control his impulses; and when he couldn't arrive at a sense of who he was or where he was going. Sam's lost years.

So here's the big question: Is it that autistic people are incapable of friendship, or is it a social problem, with neuro-typicals refusing to accept or befriend people with autism? This topic is hotly debated by autistic bloggers. The Autistic Bitch from Hell pulls no punches in this pointed blog entry: "One of the saddest autism stereotypes is the one about inability to make friends. Every now and again, a parent will say something like, 'My autistic son has never had a friend. It's part of his disability.'" Not so, she argues; the problem is "society's disability." That is, mainstream social attitudes make accepting and appreciating human diversity impossible. She goes on to chide psychologists for inventing scientific-sounding labels and throwing around half-baked pronouncements about "lack of empathy" and "lack of social skills."

So don't blame autism. Society's intolerance explains why autistic people don't have friends. Well, okay. I can't really disagree with the blame-society argument after watching Sam be ostracized in high school. No doubt about it, neuro-typical students and teachers made little or no effort to accept someone as different as Sam. How do you make friends with people who avoid you like the plague? Enough said.

Still, it's hard for me to believe that's the whole story. I mean, autistic people do have some traits that make relationships difficult. No kidding!

Consider this anecdote. For a time Sam was interested in a young woman named Stephanie who belonged to his social club. At first glance it seemed like a match made in heaven, or at least by an online dating service. Not only were they both about the same age, they were both autistic and equally talkative. So far, so good. Problem was, Stephanie hated being touched as much as Sam liked to touch. Wherever they were, Sam would reach out and immediately stroke her hand or arm.

"Please don't touch me," Stephanie would say. "I don't like to be touched."

Which prompted Sam to touch her. Again.

Which prompted Stephanie to say, "Please don't touch me." Again.

And so on.

On the other hand, it's hard to ignore hundreds of accounts written by autistic people who have been treated badly by neuro-typicals in different social situations. One of the best and most recent examples was just posted (as of this writing) on the CNN website. Written by Daniel Passantino and entitled "Autism on Campus: The Other Diversity," the personal essay presents his account of being ostracized and eventually expelled from Hunter College's Manhattan dorms. The essay begins:

"As I walked home through Central Park one afternoon — having been expelled from Hunter College's Manhattan dorms that morning — I was so emotionally drained that even the bare trees seemed vivacious by comparison. During my two months as a resident student, I'd lost 15 pounds, slept maybe five hours a night, and had constant, vivid flashbacks of my many humiliations. I spent my days as tense as a hunted animal, fearing the scornful gazes of students who shunned me like they would a person who'd committed a heinous crime. My self-esteem was shattered; when enough people look at you with disgust, it's hard not to see yourself as disgusting."

Even more poignantly, Passantino recounts his attempts to befriend other students, even to the point of following them. The result? He gets called in front of school administrators for harassing other students: "Instead of going places with students, I began getting summoned to meetings with the school staff where I'd be told 'certain students felt threatened' by me 'hanging around them,' that 'troubling stories' about me had been heard and that I'd been 'stalking people.'"

Pretty damn pathetic. But it happens all the time. I know from my experience watching Sam suffer rejection.

Sadly, after reading thousands of blog entries posted by autists, I find little mention of dating, love, romance, or marriage. Almost nothing. After reading Daniel Passantino's essay, you can understand why.

For a time I thought Sam had given up on trying to find a companion, but once he entered his mid-twenties he seemed to have a change of heart. Now he's thinking about getting back in the game. In a year or two.

Why the change? Mostly, I suspect, it's because of the influence of his friend and companion Mike, who's like a big brother. Blame Mike for introducing Sam to rap music and serious partying. "He got me all eaten up," Sam says.

A warm, friendly, extremely social 30-year-old, RogDog comes to see Sam two afternoons a week. He arrives in his red sports car, his party wagon extraordinaire. On Mondays they go to a movie and then to a restaurant, usually Champs or Appleby's. On Fridays they don't mess around. They go straight to Uno's for pizza and some serious socializing time with all their buds who work there, especially the lovely Olivia.

Lately Sam's been asking lots of questions about relationships. "How did you know Cindy was right for you?" he'll ask. Or: "How will I know when I find the right one?"

"Well, you just kind of know," I'll say, as ineptly as ever. "You like to do things with each other and spend time together. It's hard to explain, but you'll know when you meet that special someone."

"What if I've already met him? I mean her? Should I hit on her?"

Here I usually pause a moment, unsure if he's really serious or really even understands the term. He picks up a lot of sexual lingo from his rap music without really knowing what it means. Hit on?

"I guess. Sure, ask her if she wants to do something," I'll say. "Who is it?"

He'll look at me suspiciously. "Why do you want to know?"

So much for fatherly advice.

Then on another occasion he'll ask, "How do I get a woman? You know, get one to like me?"

I'll say something about being gentle and saying nice things. Sweet talk. Lots of compliments. The usual stuff.

Sam will think about that for a moment, then head for the bedroom phone. A moment later I'll hear him talking to Melissa, saying sweet nothings. "I think you're WONderful, Melissa!" he'll say.

If nothing else, he's getting good practice for when he meets the right one.

Sam's favorite day is Fabulous Friday, when he and RogDog go to Uno's. Most of the time he'll be waiting at the door or in the driveway when the red sports car zips down the street and up to our house, music blasting. Sam refers to the car as a "babe magnet."

Just last Friday, after returning from Uno's, he bragged about riding around in the babe magnet with Mike. "The babes notice me and RogDog," he said. "And we notice them, too."

"Maybe that's what I need," I said. Driving my '96 Camry with over 150,000 miles, I can't even get my wife to notice me.

Sam gave me a funny look. "Yeah, like that's gonna happen!"

Chapter 8

Self-Injury

We follow the same routine each time the head-banging occurs. It can happen suddenly, like a flash of lightning, or it can develop gradually over the course of a day until Sam finally explodes. Even if I'm in another room, I'll recognize that familiar sound: BAM! BAM! BAM! When Sam was younger, I would try to rush in and prevent him from hurting himself. But that only made things worse, sending Sam into an uncontrollable rage. Directed at me!

So now I stand back while Sam bangs his head against the wall. I try to take a Zen-like attitude. That is, I try to go to a different place in my mind, to transport myself mentally to a different realm where this is not happening. To achieve a state of dispassion. I'm getting better all the time. Sounds cold, I suppose. But without the ability to disengage in these situations I don't know how parents of autistic children could keep their sanity.

"It's okay, Sam," I say. "You're safe. You're at home."

I wait until Sam stops banging his head, until he reaches the quiet place that comes after the storm. Afterward he's calmer and usually contrite. Sometimes his body goes limp, as though he's just experienced a seizure, or a jolt of electricity. By this time he's usually bloody. He prefers to hit the top of his forehead on the corner of a wall, which leaves a nasty gash that, when healed, will become another battle scar. As if he doesn't have enough already.

As soon as I can get his attention, Sam follows me down to the Yellow Submarine. I draw him a bubble bath in his Jacuzzi tub while he tells me how sorry he is. "Did I hurt anyone?" he'll usually ask, not fully aware of what has just transpired. Again, it's like a seizure in that respect. Most of the time the answer is no, he didn't hurt anyone else. When he sinks into the water, I can see the last of the tension drain out of his body. He relaxes in the bubbles, while I pour warm water over his head, washing away the blood and plaster. If the gash on his forehead is deep, I'll wash it with a Betadine solution and cover it with a bandaid to keep it clean. Otherwise I leave it to heal on its own.

While he soaks, I'll clean up the blood, wiping down the floor and the walls upstairs. Plaster repair, if necessary, has to wait until another day.

"I'm sorry," Sam will say.

"I'm sorry, too," is always my response.

When I ask what happened, why he hit his head, he goes silent. If anything, he'll say, "Don't ask. It's just my impulses."

After his bath, he usually wants to be by himself, to watch the Weather Channel or listen to his music. As though nothing had happened. No big deal.

Though I've tried a hundred times, I've never been able to get Sam to really talk about why he bangs his head and what the banging accomplishes. I wonder if he even understands why. Just his impulses, he'll say. Nothing more.

Why do so many autistic people intentionally hurt themselves? Some bite their arms; others pull out their hair. What's the deal?

To find an answer I launched an extensive online search, reading every blog, article, and interview transcript I could find of autistic people talking about self-injury. Some patterns began to emerge. I say patterns because, like any group of people, no two autistic people are the same. But I did find some agreement, some commonalities. For example, many people commented on how their reasons for hurting themselves not only varied but evolved over time. I saw this same phenomenon in Sam, whose head-banging has changed with age and circumstance.

When Sam was little, he would rock himself to sleep, hitting his head on the sides of the bed. Sometimes when he took afternoon naps he would bonk himself into a trance-like state. Finally we had to put cushions on both sides of the bed frame, or he would develop bruises or scrapes on his forehead. A precursor of what was to come.

In her Ballastexistenz blog, Amanda Baggs refers to similar behavior on her part as "chasing oblivion." "When I was a kid, I really didn't want to exist," she explains. By banging her head she could approach unconsciousness, which seemed like non-existence. Only later did her head-banging evolve into an "impulsive action" that she could only sometimes control.

Like Baggs, Sam's head-banging seemed to become an "impulsive action" as he got older. When he banged his head it would usually come in one of two situations: when he wanted attention; or when he was overburdened by tension or anxiety. In fact, the first time Sam banged his head on the wall, I was upstairs watching television and heard him call out to have me come down and find something for him. When I said just a minute, he started banging his head on the stairway. He wanted my attention NOW! I came down to find him bloody and blaming me for not reacting soon enough.

Still today Sam will resort to head-banging if he wants, but isn't getting, our full attention. For example, if Sam's mom and I are talking intensely, or if we're paying more attention to someone else (especially one of his sisters), Sam might very well hurt himself as a way to return to the center of attention.

Other autistic people have written about this need for attention. "Sometimes I scream and head-bang just to show how handicapped I am," writes Sue Rubin in "Killing Autism Is a Constant Battle." "Heroes demand worship; autistic people demand attention."

That's Sam, in a nutshell.

Even so, tension remains Sam's primary trigger. On a day he's feeling tense, or "all eaten up" (as he says) by anxiety, I do my best to talk him down. I slow myself down and spend quiet time with him, chatting or walking, whatever he wants to do. Sometimes it works; sometimes not. Some days, it seems, he just needs to bang his head to readjust his electrical impulses or his brain chemistry, whatever head-banging accomplishes for him.

Most autistic bloggers agree that tension can lead to self-injury. Donna Williams includes head-banging in "An Outline of Language in 'My World,'" an appendix to her autobiography, *Nobody Nowhere*. She explains the purpose of her head-banging: "To fight tension and to provide a thudding rhythm in my head when my mind was screaming too loud for me to be able to hum or to repeat a hypnotic tune in order to calm down."

This brings me to a fascinating concept. Williams and many of the autistic bloggers discuss self-injury as a kind of embodied language. A form of communication that provides a second language for autistic people, much the same way that American Sign Language provides a second language for the Deaf community. So that physical behaviors (or performances, if you will) become linguistic acts, both expressing and creating meaning for those who understand the language. That's the catch, of course. Most neuro-typicals don't understand this embodied language. It takes an enormous amount of time and patience for parents and teachers to be able to "translate" expressive behaviors such as hand-flapping and head-banging. I've lived with autism over a period of almost 30 years, and I can't claim to be more than a novice at translating autistic behaviors.

Moreover, many autistic people say that, in moments of frustration (or confusion), they must rely on an embodied language to complement or even replace speech. Looked at from this perspective, it would be counterproductive for neuro-typicals to try to eliminate these expressive behaviors. If you take away the behaviors, you take away an important (sometimes the only) form of communication. You deny the autistic person the linguistic tools to express him/herself.

Michelle Dawson alludes to many of these issues in a post from her Autism Crisis blog. She recounts being asked in a documentary why she hurt herself. "What I said ... was that it (hurting myself) was my vocabulary," she writes. "Then I said that I'd worked hard all my life to learn language. This was very, very difficult and took pretty much all my resources. But I learned, and I learned two languages. Then I found out this language thing didn't work; I was not good enough at it; I somehow did it wrong. My very accurate words weren't heard."

"I hurt myself to re-establish some form of accuracy," she continues. "So while it may seem that I'm frustrated, that isn't the case ... there is an essential need to re-establish, after repeated failed communication, the existence of accuracy, or at least the possibility of accuracy, in order to continue to function at all."

Certainly, Sam has these same issues with communication, despite being verbally adept. Sometimes, out of confusion or whatever, he'll be unable to communicate his feelings. Here's a typical scenario. We'll be driving somewhere, and on the way Sam will change his mind about going. Instead of saying he doesn't want to go, he'll sit in his seat, sullen and conflicted. Finally he'll reach over and either honk the horn or hit me. Sam has a history of this behavior. Throughout junior and senior high, "Talk, don't touch!" became a mantra that all Sam's teachers repeated.

Easier said than done for someone who communicates as much by touch as by speech.

Emotions can be doubly difficult for Sam to express. This is especially true when he's sad or depressed. Once repressed, these emotions can cause anxiety and lead to head-banging.

Like most people with disabilities, Sam has low self-esteem and an acute sense of his own failures. Largely this is a reflection of how other people react to him, especially strangers. He's perfectly aware of the stigma attached to disability. And when he fails, he suffers the slings and arrows of his own bad feelings about himself.

For example, just recently Sam and I drove to a convenience store to buy him a soft drink. Sam opened his car door into the vehicle parked next to us, making a tiny nick in its paint. The owner of the vehicle made a big stink, demanding to see my insurance card and yelling at Sam. Since then, whenever we drive to a convenience store, Sam refuses to get out or even open his door. He monitors himself closely because his sense of failure is so intense.

Diagnosed with a mood disorder, Sam has frequent bouts of depression. To make matters worse, he won't talk about why he's depressed or what we can do to help. He can't get the words out. Instead, he'll punish himself. If he drops or knocks over something, he'll bonk his head on the nearest object. Depression makes any kind of communication difficult.

The more depressed Sam is, the more fragile he becomes. When he's in one of these moods I go out of my way to treat him with love and kindness. Yelling at him would be the worst thing to do. Sadly, it was during his high school years, when he battled depression daily, that Sam was yelled at most often. Yelled at by teachers, counselors, job coaches, and others. What did the yelling accomplish? Nothing. Sam would hurt himself or strike out at others.

Amanda Baggs writes about being yelled at under similar circumstances. The yelling produces a kind of dissonance or mental static that results in a failure of communication. Predictably, the yelling also triggers head-banging. Baggs relates one incident where, after repeatedly asking and failing to obtain a particular piece of information from someone she was with, she becomes frustrated and starts banging her head. When that happened, the person with her started yelling, "Listen to me!"

Baggs writes: "And the whole time I was thinking, 'I *am* listening to you, why the hell do you think I'm overloaded, lady? Now stop screaming at me or I won't be able to quit hearing you long enough to stop this.'"

You can begin to see the complexity of this issue.

Let's go back to the concept of embodied language. Is self-injury an expressive embodied language, or is it only a reaction to external factors? And to what extent can or should self-injurious behaviors be eliminated?

For Sam, head-banging can be both a language and a reaction. If he's not getting enough attention, or if something spills on the floor, he may react by banging his head. In this case his head-banging is clearly a reaction to an external event.

On the other hand, if he's confused, or if he's having bad

feelings about himself, he'll sink into a nearly catatonic depression. On those days there's nothing I can do to bring him out of his depression. He'll actually lose his power to speak, even though his negative body language makes it clear how he feels. He'll sit, silent and sullen, until an internal or external trigger sets him off. Then he'll head for the nearest wall and start banging his head.

BAM! BAM! BAM!

An embodied language? I suppose, because in those situations banging his head becomes the only way he can express himself, the only way he can break the negative mood and move on.

And this is precisely what happens. After he bangs his head, Sam begins to relax. He not only regains his power to speak, he resumes chatting as though nothing out of the ordinary had occurred.

Here's the rub. If head-banging can be considered a linguistic act, then is it fair for me to want to eliminate that behavior? Probably not, even though I would give anything for a way to stop his head-banging. I mean, head-banging can be lethal, especially for someone with a shunt. And of course I do try, encouraging him to change languages and instead talk about his feelings. I beg him to use words. To talk about whatever's bothering him.

Writing this, I'm struck by the futility of my actions.

I say this because head-banging isn't a choice, it's a need. On the bad days Sam needs to bang his head, period. Nothing I do will change that.

So when it happens I'm left standing on the sidelines watching, having to make peace with the inevitable. I comfort Sam while he bangs his head, telling him that everything will be okay, that he's safe. I never know if any of this is true, of course, but I say it anyway because I have nothing else to say. What can I give him but empty words of comfort? Once he's finished, I bath him and wash away the blood, chatting and pretending, like him, that everything's just fine.

Usually the next day I repair the walls. Over the years Sam has put many a hole in the drywall. He'll watch, listening to his portable

CD player, while I spread a drop cloth and arrange my tools: spackling compound, putty knives, and nylon mesh. For cracks and small indentations, the two-inch putty knife will work. Larger holes require the four-inch putty knife and a layer of nylon mesh, over which I spread thin layers of spackling compound top to bottom, side to side. Next day I sand and apply another thin layer, which after another 24 hours will be sanded again and finally painted.

Sam doesn't comment on the patches, which if you look close enough, remain forever visible on the walls, like the scars on his forehead.

But the walls sometimes make Sam think about himself. After watching me plaster, he'll sometimes go into the bathroom and look at himself in the mirror. It's the only time he ever looks at himself in a mirror. Ever.

"How do I look?" he'll ask, pulling a baseball cap down over his forehead.

"Good!" I say, whether or not it's true.

"Are you sure? Can you see anything?"

"Not a thing," I say.

And we put the episode behind us, like all the others, never to be mentioned again.

Chapter 9

Weatherweenie

Back in the early 1990s, before Sam took up gangsta rap, his primary interest in life was weather, the fouler the better. Fair is foul, and foul is fair, perfectly describes Sam's feelings about the weather. As an amateur meteorologist with his own weather station, Sam's motto was, "Start a running, the big one's a coming!" To this day he maintains a bookcase filled with weather videos and books left over from his weather period. Back then he preferred to watch or read about tornadoes and hurricanes, but if they weren't available, he would settle for earthquakes, cyclones, monsoons, and floods. Even a water spout or dust devil would do in a pinch, if he were desperate enough.

Hand's down, Sam's favorite video was *Storm Chaser* by storm chaser extraordinaire, Warren Faidley. Sam would always close the door of his room before booting up this particular video. We would hear him inside, playing, rewinding, and playing again the same dramatic scene over and over. After a few minutes Sam would come racing out of his room, saying, "Come watch this! The hunter becomes the hunted! The hunter becomes the hunted!" Then he would grab my hand and practically drag me into his room to watch the video.

The scene unfolds simply enough. No special effects, no story line. Just Warren Faidley talking on camera after a long day spent chasing tornados near Midland, Texas. With storms still kicking up all around him, threatening to become tornadoes, Faidley looks into the camera and deadpans, "The hunter is going to become the hunted as the night wears on."

That's heady stuff to Sam, the amateur meteorologist, especially since Warren Faidley isn't some ordinary storm chaser. No way. He's the King, a full-time professional storm chaser of mythic proportions who for over 20 years has been racing hell-bent across the Great Plains capturing killer storms on film and videotape. Hurricanes and natural disasters, too. Just take a look at this line from his website bio: "His amazing career began at age 12 after he was swept away by a flash flood. After recovering from the near drowning — he moved on to riding his bicycle into the heart of dust devils." Part meteorologist, part dare devil, and part Davy Crockett, Faidley claims to be the only person to have witnessed both an F-5 tornado and a category 5 hurricane and lived to tell the story!

Sam loved Warren Faidley. Still does. Not even the Hollywood movie *Twister* starring Helen Hunt could compete with Faidley's *Storm Chaser* video. *Twister* had too much romantic plot for Sam's liking. Plus, the Helen Hunt movie was just a bunch of special effects, whereas *Storm Chaser* was the real deal. Same for *The Wizard of Oz*, except Sam really liked the flying house Dorothy rode to the land of Oz. The flying house was really cool, better than the flying cows in *Twister*.

No, Warren Faidley's video was the gold standard, against which every other tornado/disaster movie would forever be measured. Along with the video, Sam had the accompanying book, *Storm Chaser: In Pursuit of Untamed Skies*, which he carried with him for years on vacations and summer camps until the book came unbound from too much use, only to be discarded one section at a time until nothing remained but the empty cover.

Faidley's website (stormchaser.com) provides lots of information, all of which Sam knows by heart. Just as good, the website sells books, videos, and storm chaser gear. Cool stuff like "Chase Team" caps, and T-shirts and sweatshirts imprinted with Faidley's unmistakable tornado logo. Who needs Helen Hunt when you have all this at your disposal?

Sam never ordered any storm chaser gear, but he has a desk drawer full of weather radios that people have given him over the years (gifts that keep on giving — every time the warning siren blasts!). In addition to a stack of weather calendars from every year since 1991, he has autographs and letters from most of the TV meteorologists in the Cincinnati area. Most impressively, he has a shelf packed with back issues of *Weatherwise* magazine, the unofficial publication of the American Meteorological Association. The magazine's name comes from a Benjamin Franklin homily: "Some people are weatherwise, but most are otherwise."

Everyone who's truly obsessed by weather reads *Weatherwise* magazine. We found that out the day we called to subscribe. Up until then Sam and I had picked up issues at the local bookstore. Problem was, sometimes the issues sold out as fast as Harry Potter novels. They'd be gone by the time we arrived to purchase our copy, so we'd end up driving around the city from one bookstore to another, looking for the latest issue hot off the press.

Not good, given the amount of patience Sam usually displays. So one day I took the bull by the horns and called the offices of *Weatherwise*. I needed a subscription fast, I said, because my son was a weather nut.

The woman on the other end laughed. "All our readers are weather nuts," she said. "There's even a word for them. They're called 'weatherweenies.'"

"No way," I said.

"Yep. Weatherweenies," she assured me.

"Why weatherweenies?"

"Beats me," she said. "I don't know who first coined the term, but that's what they're called. Guys obsessed by weather. They're mostly guys, you know."

I told her I didn't doubt that one bit.

She hung up before I could ask her about Benjamin Franklin. Maybe he coined the term. If weatherwise, why not weatherweenie?

Sam read every issue of *Weatherwise*, cover to cover, for over 10 years until he changed his primary allegiance from weather to rap music. Back then, he was known as the neighborhood meteorologist. People would e-mail him for his personal weather forecast. You could ask him any question about weather and expect an answer.

What was the hottest temperature ever recorded on the planet. No problem: 136.4 degrees, on Sept. 13, 1922, in El Azizia, Libya.

The hottest in the U.S.? No problem: 134 degrees, on July 10, 1913, in Death Valley, California.

The hottest in Cincinnati? No problem: 109 degrees, on July 21, 1934.

Didn't matter if you asked him about the coldest weather, the driest weather, the wettest weather, or the snowiest weather, he would have the answers.

And the Fujita Scale? Forget about it. Sam could lecture on the Fujita Scale in his sleep (in fact, I think he sometimes does, because when there's stormy weather outside, he usually hums for most of the night).

Here's the breakdown according to Sam:

F-0, minor tornado, winds up to 72 mph, hardly worth mentioning.

F-1, moderate tornado, winds 73–112 mph, just starting to get interesting.

F-2, significant tornado, winds 113–157 mph, now we're talking, as trees snap and roofs start to crumble.

F-3, severe tornado, winds 158–206 mph, grab your gumbo and hold on, as roofs and autos start to fly.

F-4, devastating tornado, winds 207–260 mph, now you're really in for it, as houses are leveled or blown down the street like tumbleweeds.

F-5, incredible tornado, winds 261–318, everything is leveled, gone!

Not many people know there's an F-6 category, called an "Inconceivable Tornado" because winds tend to be unmeasurable and damage unidentifiable. An F-6 is so inconceivable that Sam won't even go there. His imagination stops at F-5. That's enough destruction, even for Sam.

At school Sam was known as "Sam the weather man." When asked to do free writing in his English classes, he inevitably wrote weather poems. Not romantic, back to nature Wordsworthian poems about quiet pastures, shepherds, and flowers. These are stormy weather poems. Here's an example, titled "A Funnel Cloud":

> I saw a funnel cloud up in the sky
> It was very black, my oh my
> I talked to the funnel cloud
> The wind inside was loud
>
> The funnel cloud destroyed many houses
> It sucked up lots of mouses
> It picked up a girl named Nancy
> And tickled her fancy
>
> The tornado siren went off at midnight
> The moon did not shine bright
> The people ran under cover
> And they hurried for their lovers.

Not exactly Shakespeare, but you can see the intensity of Sam's focus. More like Edgar Allan Poe, I guess. I have no idea where the last line comes from? And they hurried for their lovers?

Even when asked to write in a tight, well-defined poetic form, Sam's imagination ran to severe weather. Here's one of his Haiku:

> Summer ocean waves.
> Splash against the sandy beach.
> Washing the bathers.

Sounds so pastoral, yes? Until the second stanza:

> A spring bud opens.
> Flowers blown in the closing sun.
> Bringing tornadoes.

You get the picture.

Sam was so knowledgeable about the weather that his fifth grade science teacher asked him to teach a class on meteorology, namely stormy weather. His teacher made a video, which we still have, of Sam teaching the class. He sits in the front of the room on a swivel chair, reading his list of Dos and Don'ts for tornadoes and hurricanes. As he reads from his list, he rocks his head and swivels from side to side, stopping occasionally to glance at one of his friends in the front row or to ask his teacher a weather related question. Most of the time Sam already knows the answer; he just wants to hear it from his teacher.

After Dos and Don'ts, he takes questions from the class. And the teacher.

How do supercells produce tornadoes? Well, wind shear causes rotation in a thunderstorm, then the updraft stretches the storm vertically, increasing the spin until ... RUN!

Quite a performance for a 11-year-old with no teaching experience and no degree in meteorology. Sam the weather man.

We wanted to encourage Sam's interest in meteorology, so we bought him a stack of college guides, thinking he might eventually want to consider taking a class or two at a nearby college. After pouring through the college guides for a few weeks, he made his choice: either Brevard Community College in Florida, or the University of Oklahoma. Neither was nearby, but both had highly rated meteorology programs. Sam couldn't decide between them. At Brevard he could get in a little beach time, but Oklahoma was right smack in the middle of the Tornado Corridor. How do you decide between the beach and the Tornado Corridor? It was a tough call.

Eventually, Sam chose Brevard Community College, pointing out that Florida also had a high incidence of tornadoes. He wanted us to know that he would be ready for some serious meteorology classes. In a year or two.

About this same time, we decided to take Sam on a tour of the nearest National Weather Service office in Wilmington, Ohio. We discovered, through a friend, that the NOAA facility gave public tours, on request. So we called and scheduled a tour for Sam the following week.

When tour day arrived, Sam was so psyched that he bounced up and down on the rear seat of our car all the way to Wilmington. The hour and a half drive seemed like a day and a half, given our frayed nerves. Cindy and I were exhausted when we arrived, but Sam was literally shaking with excitement, so much so that the reception-ist inside took one look at us and frowned. She excused herself, going into the rear of the building to where the National Weather Service scientists were working at their computer terminals. When she returned, she brought bad news.

"I'm sorry, but there's a storm approaching," she said. "We're unable to give you a tour at this time."

I'd noticed the darkening sky outside, but I couldn't tell if that was the real reason they wouldn't accommodate us, or if their decision had more to do with Sam being a bit different, not to mention hyper.

"What are you talking about?" I blurted out. "You don't understand, we just drove an hour and a half to get here. We SCHEDULED this!" I was almost shouting.

The woman offered a lukewarm apology, which further incensed me. But before I could finish my lecture on the inhospital-ity of government employees, Sam started pinching and hitting. The argument had made him anxious, and now his behavior had spun out of control. You didn't need to be a meteorologist to measure the atmosphere in that lobby. It was tense.

No thanks to NOAA, we managed to get Sam outside where, like a beacon of hope, the Dopler radar appeared at the end of the parking lot. I'm here to tell you that Wilmington's Dopler radar saved the day. With his interest reignited, Sam headed for the radar, a steel tower with what looked like a giant white golf ball squashed down on top of the tower.

We took several photos of Sam standing in awe before the tower, as if it were a monument, or a shrine, where weatherweenies came to worship. Or at least to dream.

So this was where all those fascinating red, yellow, green, and blue blobs on the radar screen, via NOAA online, originated? It was almost worth the three-hour trip up and back. Almost.

By the end of the 1990s, Sam had pretty much lost his obsession with weather. That's not to say he lost all interest, only that weather was no longer his primary focus. That honor belonged to rap music.

But there's more to this story, because one day I took one of Sam's discarded *Weatherwise* issues into a science and medical writing class I was teaching. I wanted to use one of the articles as an example of how to include narrative (or story telling) in a science article. After class, one of the students came up and told me her sister read *Weatherwise* magazine.

"Really," I said, surprised.

"Yeah, she's a meteorology major at the University of Oklahoma," my student said. "She's CRAZY. She spends all day driving around looking for tornadoes, and when she doesn't see one, she's ... DISAPPOINTED!"

"Go figure!" I said.

"Can you imagine?"

"I wish I could hook her up with my son — he's into the same stuff. Warren Faidley and the whole storm chasing scene."

My student laughed. "My sister says storm chasing isn't what it used to be. She says it's hard for professionals to get close anymore because of all the amateur crazies running around Oklahoma and Texas looking for tornadoes. When she does find a tornado, the roads are like one big parking lot. Emergency vehicles can't even get through, that's how bad it is."

"I had no idea."

"My sister says she won't stop until she photographs a really big tornado. I think something's wrong with her. She's addicted."

"I know what you mean," I said.

I couldn't wait to tell Sam, but when I got home that evening he seemed disinterested in the storm chasing scene, the glut of amateur thrill-seekers clogging the highways of the Tornado

Corridor and getting in the way of professionals like Warren Faidley.

"Your student goes to the University of Oklahoma?"

"No, her sister. Her sister's the storm chaser," I said.

Sam looked at me. "Did you get her phone number?"

Chapter 10

To Cure or Not to Cure

Should we accept autism as naturally occurring neurodiversity, or should we consider it a defect that needs to be cured? This debate has been raging in the autism community for many years. Taking the lead in the cure movement are two of the big three autism advocacy organizations, Autism Speaks and Cure Autism Now. The two nonprofits have recently merged into one megabucks organization run (it's important to remember) by non-autistics. Not surprisingly, their mission statements list similar goals. Autism Speaks claims to be "dedicated to funding global biomedical research into the causes, prevention, treatments, and cure for autism; to raising public awareness about autism and its effects on individuals, families, and society; and to bringing hope to all who deal with the hardships of this disorder." Cure Autism Now adds: "A cure is closer than we thought — in time for this generation."

The two organizations (along with the Autism Society of America) worked long and hard to persuade Congress to pass the 2006 Combating Autism Act. Their lobbying efforts included a public relations campaign to enlist the support of other autism advocates and organizations, encouraging them to write individual members of Congress and urge passage. The act, finally signed into law by President George W. Bush on Dec. 19, 2006, will increase funding for autism-related research at the National Institutes of Health from $110 million in 2006 to $132 million this year and to $210 million by 2011. On signing the bill, Bush echoed the pro-cure rhetoric:

"For the millions of Americans whose lives are affected by autism, today is a day of hope. The Combating Autism Act of 2006 will increase public awareness about this disorder and provide enhanced federal support for autism research and treatment. By creating a national education program for doctors and the public about autism, this legislation will help more people recognize the symptoms of autism. This will lead to early identification and intervention, which is critical for children with autism. I am proud to sign this bill into law and confident that it will serve as an important foundation for our Nation's efforts to find a cure for autism."

This all sounds good, but what does "cure" mean? It's not clear in Bush's remarks or in the information you find on the organizational websites. Let's postpone this discussion and first give equal time to the anti-cure position.

By and large, most autistic-run organizations and activists reject the idea of curing autism. To them, curing autism means eliminating autistic people. During the Combating Autism Act debate, the autistic blogosphere maintained a united front against the act. In fact, bloggers circulated "Combating the Combating Autism Act" form letters that could be sent to members of Congress urging them to vote against the bill. For example, in her Lisa-Jedi blog, Lisa refers to the act as a "travesty" intended not to help but to "eradicate" autistic people. She includes a sample letter that reads in part:

"I urge you to not support S. 843, the Combating Autism Act of 2005, when it comes before the U.S. Senate in the coming weeks. This legislation, while it is important in awareness, is not conducive to supporting the individual with autism. Instead, it would likely lead to glorified genocide, under the guise of being good for the society."

The letter goes on to argue that the focus of the legislation needs to change so that funding goes to help currently living autistic people and not to research that will eradicate them. As currently drafted, the legislation sends the message that autistic people are not "acceptable" to society and thus have to be eliminated. But by curing autism, there would be a loss of creative and unique individuals who contribute in their own way to the social good.

The letter concludes: "We, the autistic people, their families and friends, beg you to reconsider supporting this act if you already do so. No justification can be made for eliminating a vein of inspiration to many who surround us, as we are told, and many of us do not realize how truly 'refreshing' most other individuals of society find us."

Ignoring the last line (refreshing?), the letter makes three points that are typical of the anti-cure position. First, the act does not support real, living autistic people; that is, it does not fund supports, accommodations, and services that would make their lives better. Second, a cure, whatever form it takes, will almost certainly be the equivalent of genocide against autistic people. Third, the act will result in treatments (if not a cure) that will erase or obliterate the distinct personalities of autistic folks. Each of these critiques needs elaboration.

First, the act does not address the actual services that most autistic people need. Anyone who's ever had a family member affected by autism knows that in order to live independently (or even semi-independently) the autistic person needs a community, a network of helpers who provide a variety of services. These services can include anything from transportation, housecleaning, cooking, shopping, medical care, whatever. At present it's difficult, in some places impossible, to get state Medicaid waivers that will pay for these services so that autistic people can live in apartments or houses (and NOT group homes or institutions). The problem? Funding. So why not allocate at least some of the Combating Autism Act's millions to providing services for living, breathing people with autism?

Second, curing autism equals eliminating autistic people. The Autistic Bitch from Hell responded to the passage of the Combating Autism Act by declaring war. Now there's a new battlefield in the United States, she insists. "If you're a rich American who has ridiculously medieval prejudices about autistic people being soulless empty shells," she writes, "you can brag about how successfully you've put us on the brink of the largest genocide ever committed." She also blames influential media executives for spreading "hateful prejudices" far and wide.

Most autistic bloggers share this pessimistic view, using words like eugenics and genocide to drive home their points. An exaggeration? Perhaps, but if you look at the recent history of biomedical research in the United States since the $3 billion Human Genome Project, you'll notice that the HGP has failed to produce its much-promised genetic "cures." Since safe and effective gene therapy does not yet and may never exist, the only way to "cure" or eliminate genetic diseases such as Down or Fragile X syndromes is through screening embryos before implantation and fetuses before birth, then discarding and aborting those that show evidence of the specific genetic conditions. One telling statistic that appears frequently in the autistic blogosphere is that today, thanks to embryonic and prenatal screening, between 80 and 90 percent of Down people are eliminated before birth.

No doubt most of the money provided by the Combating Autism Act will go to fund research into the genetic causes of autism. In March 2007, the Autism Genome Project Consortium, which includes over 50 institutions in North America and Europe, released the results of a five-year study of autism genetics in 1,600 families. Their research linked several chromosomal regions and at least one gene (neurexin-1) to an increased risk of developing autism. Biomedical workers often talk about the "therapy" that will eventually result from this and similar research into autism genetics. Such talk sounds promising, but when you consider what the word "therapy" actually means, you come way with a lot of questions and a healthy dose of skepticism.

Look, for example, at a typical article in the prestigious journal *Science*, the official publication of American Association for the Advancement of Science (AAAS), on promising new research into the genetic causes of autism. The author, Ken Garber, writes: "The hope is that most cases of autism are caused by just a few strongly acting genes, rather than many weak genes in concert. Simpler genetics would accelerate understanding of the disorder, as well as facilitate *early diagnosis* and *genetic counseling*, and provide more discrete targets for therapy" (my italics).

From the context, it's clear that by "therapy" Garber means genetic screening (thus the need for early diagnosis and genetic counseling). As so many of the bloggers insist, genetic screening leads directly and inexorably to genetic cleansing.

Don't get me wrong, I'm not arguing against choice. Every prospective parent has to make his/her own decision. My point is that a "cure" for autism is likely to be yet another screening test that will promote the elimination of autism affected embryos and fetuses. This is hardly the magic wand that's envisioned by all the smiley-face rhetoric of the pro-cure organizational websites.

Not only that, but sometimes choice works better in theory than in practice. Increasingly today, prospective parents feel pressured to terminate pregnancies that will result in "problem" babies that will "burden" society. Princeton Bioethics Professor Peter Singer (and many others) have written extensively about the ethics of abortion, euthanasia, and infanticide for lives not "worth living." This attitude is echoed in the October 2003 report of the President's Council on Bioethics, *Beyond Therapy: Biotechnology and the Pursuit of Perfection*. (Curiously, the title was later changed to *Biotechnology and the Pursuit of Happiness*). Chapter 2, "Better Children," contains the following rather blunt passage: "Third, the practice of prenatal screening has established as a cultural norm (or at least as a culturally acceptable norm) a new notion about children: the notion that admission to life is no longer unconditional, that certain conditions or traits are disqualifying. To be sure, parents confronted with the painful decision whether or not to abort an affected fetus may feel deeply divided and moved by considerations on both sides of the issue, but there appears to be a growing consensus, both in the medical community and in society at large, that a child-to-be should meet a certain (for now, minimal) standard to be entitled to be born."

Minimal standard? Sounds very much like old-fashioned eugenics. The difference is that today, thanks to biotechnology, those who have "disqualifying" conditions are eliminated before birth as opposed to after.

The third blogger critique of the Combating Autism Act involves the potential loss of autistic personalities. They argue that the treatments or cures that come out of research funded by the act will likely erase the distinctive personalities of autistic people. Here's Joseph in his Natural Variation blog: "To cure autism ... would entail turning an autistic person into a neurotypical person, and not just helping the person work around some of the liabilities of autism." According to Joseph, being cured would mean being transformed into a completely different person with different dreams, talents and interests. He concludes: "Being cured of autism is therefore akin to ceasing to exist."

In their opposition to a cure, autistic bloggers share common ground with Deaf culture, which in general rejects any proposed cure for deafness. The more militant members of the Deaf community refuse to use Cochlear implants or even speech (as we've seen in recent events at Gallaudet University, where students and faculty forced the resignation of a speaking president). Not only does Deaf culture have its own customs and values, it has its own language (American Sign Language, or ASL). In point of fact, many deaf people don't consider themselves disabled and have no need for a cure, thank you very much.

In this debate I find myself in a middle position of sorts. Like most autistic bloggers, I suspect this new research will produce only more screening tests to eliminate embryos and fetuses that might develop autism. What would a so-called cure for autism look like if not a screening test? Are we talking about gene therapy, a $3 billion pipe dream? Or are we talking about a vaccine or a medication? What?

On the other hand, if the research does result in new treatments or pharmaceuticals that can improve the lives of autistic people, why not support it? I'm not ready to reject medical science out of hand. I want to see the results.

That's my view, but I recognize the passion of the anti-cure movement. For those involved, the issue isn't theoretical; it's personal. Visceral.

To illustrate, let me tell you about a conversation I have periodically with Sam, who's acutely aware of his disabilities (and vulnerabilities).

On a day when he's feeling particularly thoughtful, he'll ask, "Would you change anything about me, if you could?"

"What do you mean?" I'll say, even though I know full well what he means.

"You know ... take away all my problems?"

His question is fraught with emotion. He thinks I'm disappointed in him because he's disabled. In moments like these I realize the weight of the emotional and psychological baggage he carries on his shoulders.

Still, I'm honest with Sam. I tell him I might change some of his self-destructive behaviors but that I would never want to change who he is.

Usually that's the end of our conversation. Last time, though, I asked a question of my own. "Why? Do you still wish you didn't have disabilities?"

He thought about it for a moment. "Not so much anymore."

If I could wave a magic wand over my son and "cure" him by taking away his autism, thereby making his life easier, I suppose I would. But here's the rub: would my magic wand also take away Sam's personality? I would never want to change Sam's funny, feisty personality.

Even at the age of 26, issues of identity are difficult for Sam to talk about. You can understand why. I mean, what we're born with is who we are. Yes?

Indeed, identity issues are at the heart of the pro-cure/anti-cure debate. Though the bloggers I mentioned above tend to be united in their opposition to a cure, the larger autistic community does not share their unanimity. This was evident in an recent exchange between two prominent autistic activists: Sue Rubin, a spokesperson for facilitated communication, and Cal Montgomery, a writer for *Ragged Edge* magazine. Rubin has consistently supported the idea of a cure for autism, arguing that "high-functioning" autistic people (or those who have Asperger's) generally reject the need for a cure because they can "pass for normal," while "low-functioning" autistic people (like herself) can't pass and are therefore much more sympathetic to the pro-cure position.

"As a low-functioning autistic person who is still really awash in autism, I am actually aligned with the cure group, although I will not personally benefit if a cure is found," Rubin writes. "Low-functioning people are just trying to get through the day without hurting, tapping, flailing, biting, screaming, etc. The thought of a gold pot of a potion with a cure really would be wonderful."

To Rubin, autism is something she has, a "genetic anomaly," a negative attribute that she wishes could be removed. "Killing autism [however momentarily] lets me enjoy a life," she writes.

Cal Montgomery comes down on the other side of the cure issue in "Defining Autistic Lives," her review of the documentary film about Rubin, *Autism Is a World*. First, she disputes Rubin's analysis of the high-functioning/low-functioning divide. "If you use Rubin's definition, I'm low-functioning: I don't speak," Montgomery writes. "Like Rubin, I use augmentative communication. Like her, I engage in self-injurious behavior (SIB)."

The real divide, Montgomery argues, is between those who consider themselves autistic people and those, like Rubin, who see themselves as people "with" autism (something "awful" in Rubin's terms).

"I, on the other hand, see myself as an autistic person," Montgomery writes. "The behaviors and experiences that get me labeled 'autistic' are, I think, part of me. I want to change some of them, sure. I want to not hurt myself (or at least manage to only do it when I'm alone), and it frustrates me that I am getting worse at that. I want to always manage to get my helmet on before I hit my head on something. I want enough motor control to type on my communication device and navigate my powerchair whenever I'm out."

Montgomery enlists the support of Amanda Baggs, who adds: "Autism is not a peripheral feature that I can discard." Baggs points out that autism shapes her entire life; that is, her mind, her personality, her senses, her values, her goals, her dreams, and so on. Autism is a significant part of what makes her and her closest friends unique, she writes.

A powerful argument, no doubt about it.

When I look at Sam, I can't help but agree with Cal Montgomery and Amanda Baggs. Certainly he would be categorized as low-functioning, given his physical impairments and behavioral problems. And certainly his autism is not a peripheral feature; it's an essential part of what makes him Sam. To cure Sam would be to change him into someone else. A different person. An imposter.

That's not to say I'm an essentialist. I don't reduce Sam (or anyone else) to his autism. I don't call him an autistic. He's not autism, he's an autistic person. There's an enormous difference.

But autism is such an important part of Sam's personality that, if his autism were somehow miraculously cured, his personality would be irrevocably changed.

Sam would no longer be Sam.

And yet, I'll have to admit, the thought of a cure holds a powerful attraction, even for a skeptic like me. If not a cure, then how about new treatments or medications that would somehow eliminate Sam's aggressive and self-destructive behaviors, that would allow him to better cope with daily living and make his life easier? What parent could object to that?

You see why I'm conflicted.

At the moment, because I'm a skeptic, I would settle for more services and community supports. Good luck with that.

Here's the bottom line. If a miraculous cure did appear, I would want Sam to decide whether he wanted to be cured and risk losing his personality. Some days, I think he would choose the cure. Other days I'm not so sure. He seems happy and content to be who he is. And ... if I'm honest with myself, most days I'm happy and content he's who is. Come what may.

So I don't know. It's a touchy subject, identity.

In closing, I'll defer to the Autistic Bitch from Hell. Who else? On her website, she has a photo of herself with her back to the camera. She wears a T-shirt that shouts "Cure This!" with an arrow pointing down at you know what.

"Yeah, I'm talking to you, dude," she writes, meaning the paranoid curebie who's getting all stressed out about the devastating autism epidemic that will destroy life on the planet. "The psychologists who have been working on the DSM-V decided to add some new disorders. Not to upset you or anything, dude, but it looks like you might meet the diagnostic criteria for one of them, Apocalyptic Melodrama Disorder."

It seems the symptoms of "Apocalyptic Melodrama Disorder" include anxiety, irrational fear, and impairment of the ability to think rationally about news reports.

Enough said.

Chapter 11

Things We Do

Sam says he might want to find a job. In a year or two.

He says he might want to take a college class. In a year or two.

Meanwhile, he hangs. That's not to say he's idle. Hardly. All day long he's busy keeping time. He's the timekeeper. He never goes anywhere without his watch, which he checks every few minutes, from the moment he gets out of bed until he crashes at the end of the day. No matter what he's doing or where he happens to be, Sam can tell you the time of day.

He times the mail delivery Monday through Saturday. He times the arrival of the garbage truck Monday morning. Usually he's outside or in the garage waiting with his watch.

When one of his companions arrives a few minutes late, Sam lets them know. "What happened?" he'll ask. "Why are you late?"

Sam expects everyone to be exactly on time. If he can do it, why not everyone else?

In addition to being the timekeeper, he's also the weatherman. He can tell you the weather forecast for today or for the next seven days, your choice. He watches the local weather radar channel on TV whenever his busy schedule allows. If the weather gets dicey, he taps into the online NOAA website to get the latest watches and warnings. He's no slouch. He works hard at what he does. He prides himself on always knowing the time and weather forecast.

Don't get me wrong. Sam's no workaholic. When break time arrives promptly at 2 P.M., he's off to Wendy's or McDonald's for fries and Coke. Nothing comes between Sam and his break, not even his obsessions with time and weather.

Here's my best story. One spring day a couple of years ago we were hanging, as per our routine. Sam was busy monitoring a tornado watch for our county. But at the stroke of 2 P.M. he came upstairs and reported for break.

So we got into the car and took off, even though the sky had turned the color of India ink. Halfway to McDonald's our local tornado sirens started blaring. No kidding. That's when I noticed there wasn't another car on the road. Not one.

"Should we turn around?" I asked.

Sam checked his watch. "Nope. Party on!" he said, and pointed straight ahead.

At McDonald's we found ourselves the only customers. I'd never seen the McDonald's parking lot empty, ever! Sam wanted to go through the drive-thru so he could get quickly back to his computer.

But when we pulled up to the speaker, sirens still blaring, we heard dead silence at the other end. Eventually a meek voice asked, "Can I take your order?"

We drove around to the window and waited. Again, no one. Finally a teenager poked his head up over the window, below which he'd been crouching. He stuck his head out the window and looked up at the sky. Then he quickly took our money, gave us our fries and Coke, and ducked back down behind the window.

RRRRRRRRRRRRRRNNNNNNNNNN! followed us all the way home.

I was relieved when we made it back home, but Sam didn't blink an eye. He finished munching his fries, then took off for his computer to check the latest models.

That's a true story.

Sam measures out his day in 30-minute segments, much like the character Hugh Grant played in the movie *About a Boy*. Half-hour increments. Half a unit here, half a unit there.

He gets up promptly at 6 A.M., eats breakfast at 7 A.M., and takes his morning meds at 8 A.M. When 9 A.M. comes, he wants his shower (or bath, if it's cold that day). Between times he listens to his portable CD player, rapping at the kitchen table or downstairs in his pad.

At 10 A.M. Sam goes shopping. By then he's bored and wants to get out of the house. We go to Kroger to buy groceries or to Best Buy to pick up some CDs. Just what he needs, more CDs. Sam has over a hundred rap CDs as well as a few Beatles and Beach Boys discs to please the old folks he hangs around with on occasion. Just to humor us.

On our last trip to Best Buy Sam picked up a copy of the Beach Boys Greatest Hits, because one of his older companions has it on tape and plays it for Sam when they're driving around. Good Vibrations, that's their theme.

Except Sam felt a little embarrassed to be seen walking up to the counter at Best Buy with a Beach Boys CD. He knows most of the clerks; they're all about his age and definitely NOT Beach Boys types. "Here," you carry it, he said.

But when we got to the counter he fessed up. "Hi! I don't usually buy Beach Boys music, I like rap!" he said to the young clerk.

She laughed. It must have been the first time she'd served someone who apologized for what they were buying.

"I'm buying it for a friend of mine," Sam continued. "He's old. He likes this stuff." Sam shook his head, as if to assure her that he had better taste.

She nodded in agreement.

Since I was outnumbered, I kept my mouth shut. I happen to like the Beach Boys.

Other than Kroger and Best Buy, Sam refuses to shop. He hates buying clothes at the mall, which means I have to buy all his clothes for him, when he's not with me. I'm afraid Sam will never be much of a consumer.

Back home, Sam eats lunch at 11 A.M. Precisely. He cooks hot dogs or grilled cheese sandwiches. That's the extent of his culinary skills. Some people might consider that a rather limited menu, but not Sam. He WANTS hot dogs or chilled cheese sandwiches. Every day.

For Sam, the hard part of the day comes after lunch. He doesn't have much to do until his companions arrive. We go for walks when the weather permits, but that's not much of an outing. I try to schedule someone every day, because if he's stuck with me all day long he gets bored out of his mind. That can throw Sam into a major depression, which can lead to all sorts of bad things, including a meltdown. Sam likes his companions. I'll do in a pinch, but he likes variety on his social platter. Who can blame him?

Nearly every evening Sam goes out to dinner with one of his companions. He goes to movies once or twice a week. Back home, he listens to music or watches movies on his DVD player until bedtime. His current favorites are *Van Wilder, The Rise of Taj, Accepted, Harold and Kumar go to White Castle, Slackers, Old School,* and *School of Rock.* He likes *Borat,* sort of, but the naked wrestling scene grosses him out every time. You can see the pattern here. Sam likes comedies about slackers, good-natured slackers who always seem to get themselves in trouble. Sam likes to think of himself as a slacker, but he's much too tightly wound to be a true slacker.

Come 9 P.M., Sam wants his nightly meds. Then he's ready for bed at 9:30 give or take a few minutes either way.

That's his day, every day of the week, every day of the month. He likes his routine.

And actually, looking into the future, the routine he's established will make it easier for him to live semi-independently with helpers, if and when a state Medicaid waver comes through. He would need someone in the morning, to help with breakfast, shower, and lunch. Then someone in the evening, just to get him settled for the night, or to help with dinner if he hasn't gone out. In addition to his buds, of course. He would still need outings and recreation. But I'm hopeful. His needs aren't so great that one or two helpers couldn't get him through the day.

Some days I'll find myself wishing Sam would be more active in the community. Find a job or take a class at any of the nearly college branch campuses. Over the years he's been offered many jobs at the various restaurants he frequents, from Starbuck's to Uno's. Menial jobs, for a couple of hours at a time, but with people he knows and likes. Why, he could be a pizza sampler and house meteorologist at Uno's. That's my standing joke. But Sam always says the same thing. Maybe in a year or two I'll be ready.

I guess Sam works hard enough at just keeping himself together. Having a job would overload him to the point of meltdown.

Plus, he's had bad experiences with work. One job coach at school assigned him to break down boxes since that was all people like him with "reduced potential" were capable of doing. Another threatened to kick his ass if he didn't operate a paper shredder properly. Once Sam dropped a tray of cookies on a work-study outing and got so flustered at people yelling that he pulled down his pants and pretended to pee on the job. He might have won an Academy Award that day for over-the-top acting, a la Marlon Brando or Jack Nicholson.

Still, I worry. Not so much because of money. He collects SSI and has state Medicaid. In addition, he'll have a small discretionary trust fund that we set up for him.

No, I worry about the lack of social opportunities that work would provide. How will he meet people? Where will he find future friends or roommates? Where will he find a potential companion?

I recall one very telling post by Joel Smith on his NTs Are Weird blog. He recounts how his life has changed for the better, partly because of his job. His major problem is still "loneliness," but it's not as bad as it once was, he confesses. "I love my job, and my boss is very easy to work for."

I keep thinking: this could be Sam.

My bad, I suppose. Not everyone has to work. Blogs written by other autistic people make this same point. Some of them work. Some do art. Some make music. Some write blogs and maintain websites. Others hang. Whatever makes them happy. And so what if neuro-typicals don't approve? That's their problem.

"Autistic children are quite good at unconsciously knowing and doing what makes them happy," writes Spockette in her blog, Misadventures from a Different Perspective. "If a child is happy spinning in circles, then by all means let them spin in circles. There is no malice in the act, no desire to make others uncomfortable."

This ability continues into adulthood, Spockette argues. Problems occur when neuro-typicals object to the activities that make autistic people happy, when they subject autistic people to the pressure of normalization.

I know all that, and yet I wish Sam had more opportunities for socialization. Problem is, he usually says no to whatever I suggest. I've learned the hard way that I can't organize outings for him. He has to first decide he wants to do something. Usually he finds my suggestions corny. A Valentines Day dance sponsored by our county MRDD?

"BORING!" he'll say.

And so it goes. Whatever I propose, BORING!

Sam has a hard time during the winter months when he can't get outside. During those long, dreary months his mood darkens like the heavy clouds that roll into the Ohio River Valley. He loses his *mojo*. When I think about it, all his major meltdowns have occurred between the months of October and March. Something about the light. He needs sunshine and fresh air even more than most people.

But in summer, Sam comes alive. He's a hothouse flower. He loves to sit outside on the deck listening to his music or shooting the breeze with his companions. Warm weather allows him to walk on the neighborhood trails. He goes for walk-talks, as he calls them, talking with his companions and the neighbors he meets on the trail. Most walkers in our neighborhood have known Sam for years. He's held their hands, looked deeply into their eyes, and asked them weather questions. Or pizza questions. Everyone knows Sam's agenda.

Summer brings two of Sam's favorite activities: Cincinnati Reds baseball games and outdoor music festivals. We've gone to Reds games regularly since Sam was two years old. He likes baseball, the only sport he really cares for, because the game is slow enough for him to follow, given his visual impairments. And also because he played T-ball in the Challenger Division of Little League for many years, even though he didn't play so much as talk about his usual subjects. For that, he earned the baseball nickname of Stormin' Sammy.

When we go to Reds games, we sit in pricey seats halfway between home plate and the Reds dugout. Cost doesn't matter to me as much as being close enough for Sam to see. Not that he pays much attention to the game. He's usually focused on his hot dog and Coke, or wanting another hot dog and Coke. Most of the ushers know us by now. They joke with Sam about the game or the "bums" on the field.

Let's face it, the Reds haven't exactly been world beaters in recent years.

Usually about the 6th or 7th inning, when he's exhausted his hot dog fund, Sam will say, "This game is BORING!"

"You can say that again," one of the ushers will say. Or: "Just wait. It'll get worse."

Still, Sam loves going to the ballpark. Baseball has become a summer ritual, only topped by his favorite outdoor music festivals.

Sam goes to most of the dozen or so festivals held every summer in Cincinnati. From Fringe Fest to Octoberfest, Sam's there and definitely not square. He loves the food, the drink, and most of all the music. Except for Country, he'll dance to just about anything. And I mean dance. He gets down, a la John Travolta. "Staying Alive" could be his summer theme song.

Sam's favorite local group is a Zydeco band that plays funky Cajun music. We're like groupies, reconnecting with the band at least two or three times every summer. The lead singer, who wears a remote mike and plays the accordion, comes out to dance with Sam on occasion.

One evening two summers ago we heard them play on the levee downtown overlooking the Ohio River. It was a fairly sedate crowd of onlookers until Sam arrived, feeling friskier than usual. Leave it to Sam to break the ice. When he kicked up his heels, everyone started clapping and tossing Mardi Gras beads at him. He left with several new strands of Mardi Gras beads and his reputation as a party animal intact.

Go to any summer festival here and you just might see Sam dancing. You'll even find him cutting loose at the most famous of all local festivals, Octoberfest Zinzinnati. German om-pah-pah music might be a far cry from his beloved rap and hip-hop, but even Sam can't resist the World's Largest Chicken Dance, held every year on the last day of the festival!

For pure spectacle, served with lots of kitsch, you can't beat Octoberfest Zinzinnati. Where else can you see 20,000 drunks wearing chicken hats and humming into kazoos attempt the exacting moves of the Chicken Dance? Quite a sight: arms waving, elbows flapping, hands clapping ... a little bit of this, a little bit of that, that's what it's all about. Then the 20,000 bawdy ballerinas head for the nearest beer stand to recharge.

Each year Sam dances the Chicken Dance with a well-known celebrity brought in to lead the dance. His favorite, hands down, was Verne Troyer (aka Mini-Me), who breezed into town to orchestrate the 2002 festivities. Mini-Me, all 32 inches of him, showed up wearing an orange Hawaiian shirt and accompanied by two *Austin Powers* go-go dancers. He was riding a wave of popularity after his *Austin Powers: Goldmember* movie.

"Where's Dr. Evil?" Sam wanted to know.

"Maybe next year," someone in the crowd said.

Meanwhile, on stage, Mini-Me quaffed a German beer from a mini-mug, then declared he was ready, let the music begin.

Sam tooted his kazoo and flapped his wings as loud and hard as anyone in the crowd.

"Now," Mini-Me said, after the chickens had quieted down. "I did one of your dances, you do one of MINE!"

And with that, the *Austin Powers* theme song blared from the speakers on stage. Mini-Me and the go-go dancers got down, twisting and mugging for the crowd.

"YEAH! THAT'S BETTER!" Sam yelled, handing me his kazoo.

Chapter 12

Family Relations

You don't need to be a psychiatrist to know that families with autistic members generally have issues. Serious issues.

So when Cindy saw a short article in the *New York Times* on this very subject, she decided to use it to start a family discussion. Not that the article was terribly informative; it wasn't. In fact, the article is utterly predictable in that it reinforces the worst stereotypes about autism, as you can probably tell from its headline: "For Siblings of the Autistic, A Burdened Youth." As I've said before, using the adjective autistic as a noun essentializes the condition, reducing the person to the condition. The value-loaded word "burdened" also has an exclusively negative effect, constructing the autistic person as a profound drag on his/her stressed-out and overwhelmed siblings. So the headline effectively telegraphs the bleak message that follows.

The author, Jane Gross, writes: "Siblings of children with disabilities carry the burden of extra responsibility and worry for the future, though they are also enriched by early lessons in compassion and familial love [thank you for including something positive!]. But autism, a brain disorder that affects communication and social interaction, is in a class by itself in the heavy toll it takes on siblings, according to educators, therapists and a dozen scientific studies."

A class by itself? Heavy toll?

Cindy hoped Sam's two older sisters would pick up on the limitations of the one-sided article. For example, Gross mentions the existence of a dozen scientific studies on the burdened sibling issue but fails to provide any specifics about the results. Do these studies measure short-term effects, long-term effects, or what? Gross does include interviews with three "experts" on sibling support issues, but for the most part they point out the obvious: that siblings don't get as much attention as the autistic child, and that they sometimes internalize the anger and frustration of the parents trying to cope with the emotional needs of the family. There's nothing new here. You can find the same sentiments on websites like Autism Speaks.

The article becomes more compelling when Gross recounts her experience sitting in on several support groups in the New York area, where she listens to two dozen children age 5–11 talk openly about the difficulties of having an autistic brother or sister. With one or two exceptions, their litany of complaints seems legitimate (let's forget about the three boys who gripe about not being able to talk sports with their autistic brothers ... such deprivation!). For example, they complain that their autistic brothers and sisters are demanding, rigid, uncompromising, uncommunicative, and indifferent to affection. One young girl talks about being constantly tired, because her autistic sister was often awake and on the prowl at night; another talks about her fear of being left alone to "watch" her autistic brother. Probably the most common sibling complaint is that their needs always come second, after the needs of the autistic child. Their responses seem honest and unrehearsed.

No question that the children have reason to feel the way they do about their family situations. Everything they say rings true to my experience. The problems are real. Every autistic family negotiates these same tough issues every single day. The result, as these children demonstrate, are a lot of very stressed and unhappy people.

But here's the thing. These are children, none of them older than the age of 11. How will they feel in five, 10, or 20 years? Will their experience living with and in some cases caring for an autistic brother or sister make them more caring adults, or will it emotionally cripple them for life? Will they be empowered by experiencing neurodiversity at such a young age, or will they be paralyzed, incapacitated, unable to make a life for themselves? There are long-term questions here that are more important than how these particular children feel at the moment. Unfortunately, the Gross article doesn't address the more important questions. Instead, it demonstrates the obvious: that families with autistic members live with lots of stress.

These are the kinds of questions Cindy wanted to ask Sam's sisters, both of whom are strong, independent, successful women with both careers and loving relationships. Sam's oldest sister is a social worker in the Boston area; his youngest sister has just finished a Ph.D. in Art History at the University of California, Santa Barbara, and is currently doing a Post Doc in Switzerland. Both sisters have done well for themselves and certainly can't claim to have been held back in life because they grew up in an family with disabilities. Hadn't their balance, hard work, and general competence been fostered by living with disability? Hadn't they learned from us what Cindy referred to as an "ethical stance," or the responsibility of caring for others who have greater needs?

As parents of them as well as Sam, we hoped they would have a more positive, accepting attitude than the *New York Times* article.

As it turns out, we discovered that 10 or 15 years distance doesn't necessarily resolve all issues or heal all wounds. Sam's youngest sister, who's 33, fired the first salvo. While admitting that she and her sister were "strong, well-adjusted women with 'healthy' and 'loving' outlooks," she asked, "but how would you really know otherwise? None of us are really close enough to know each other that well. We don't have the luxury of close relationships."

Point taken. We see Sam's sisters once or twice a year. Generally, we visit them, because when they come home it's difficult for them to "deal" with Sam, who tends to be jealous of his older, more accomplished sisters.

She acknowledged that Sam had enriched her life. "Sam has made us realize how to love more unconditionally, be more tolerant of the world, be more patient, more willing to share and see things from multiple perspectives," she said. "But he has also, to a large extent, cost us parents" because "we live in a situation where Sam IS the family and Sam dictates what happens. Maybe that's what living with a disabled person is all about...."

Because of Sam, she said, no one in the family has been able to lead a "normal" life.

Ouch! That hurts. Is that really what living with a disabled person is all about ... the disabled person's needs overwhelming the family and obliterating the possibility of a "normal" life? Hmmm.

Then Sam's older sister, who's 39, joined the discussion, also dropping the (other) N word. It wasn't "normal" of us to be so focused on Sam's needs, or for the family to get together so infrequently. In effect, Sam was holding us "prisoner." "But I question the sanity of your current stance at this point of not seriously looking into alternative living situations for Sam," she said. "I don't understand how putting him into an institutional setting would be any reflection of a failing on your part."

So, let's see, institutionalizing Sam would provide for more family togetherness (except for Sam, of course). Furthermore, institutionalizing Sam would allow the rest of us to be "normal." Yes?

It's hard to underestimate the power (for some people, the allure) of normality. I'm talking here about the normative American family, a creation of the media and Madison Avenue (and of certain politicians and other demagogues). But here's the thing: the normative American family is only a myth, a fiction. In reality, there isn't a "normal" American family, just as there isn't any particular set of "family values." Instead, there are different families with different values and different norms. That's what diversity means.

Neither of Sam's sisters acknowledged or addressed the ethical issues involved in the decision to care — or not care — for people with greater needs. Only that it wouldn't be a failure on our part if we institutionalized Sam. From our point of view, placing Sam in an institution or a typical group home would be a failure. Not that we don't want Sam to live semi-independently, away from us. We do. In fact, we've worked hard over the years to build Sam's confidence and to foster his independence. Living in the Yellow Submarine, his basement apartment, has been a successful first step. We hope his next move will be to an enlightened community where he can live in his own apartment or condo supported by state Medicaid waiver and where he will have whatever services he needs.

Placing Sam in an institution certainly wouldn't make us "normal," whatever normal means. If Sam were placed in such a place, we would worry about him day and night. Emotionally, psychologically, it would be much harder on us than actually living with him. You can't simply erase a family member and declare your freedom. There's no such thing as a clean break when it comes to letting go of your child. And that's the truth. Our truth.

Maybe that's what it comes down to: different truths for different people. Sam's sisters have every right to feel the way they do. We understand their feelings because we lived through the difficult early years with them, often sharing their stress and unhappiness. We stayed with Sam because we felt an ethical responsibility to care for him, but we never expected or demanded that Sam's sisters stay to help. In fact, we supported and encouraged them to create their own lives, wanting them to feel empowered and independent, not restricted by our family situation. And they haven't been restricted or limited in any way, other than not getting as much attention as they wanted over the years.

So we were surprised, and somewhat disappointed, that Sam's sisters didn't understand our ethical stance. Not that they should necessarily be in agreement. They have to make their own decisions and judgments according to their own sense of ethics. We've never attempted to dictate our own ethics. We just wanted them to understand and support our decision to do what we felt obligated to do.

The funniest thing about our exchange occurred one night when Sam heard us talking about his sisters and their response. He didn't know what we were talking about, just that his sisters were the topic of conversation, not him. He started yelling, trying to get our attention. "You guys don't give me enough attention!" he yelled. "I want some attention!"

And there you have it. Every child wants more attention, so how can a parent win?

When we shared this anecdote with Sam's sisters, neither was amused.

So, having learned that I had failed to give ALL my children sufficient attention, I consulted the bloggers to get their read on the situation. To get a fresh perspective. As you might expect, they weren't terribly sympathetic to "whining" siblings. Their message: you can walk away from autism anytime you want, I can't. So stop bellyaching.

Here's Kassiane Montana writing in her Rett Devil blog about a different (yet another!) *New York Times* article on the plight of siblings. She titles her post, "Siblings in the NYT. Ugh." It begins: "Everyone knows, intuitively, that having a family member who is 'different' can be difficult. So why did we need to hear siblings whining (again)? Everyone has sympathy for the poor deprived siblings of autistic and other disabled kids anyway, reading them piss and moan about how their autistic brother or whoever embarrasses them is not how I want to start my day."

Well, guess what, neuro-typical siblings aren't that easy to live with either, Kassiane goes on to say. NT siblings are loud, they're unpredictable, and they hang around with loud and unpredictable friends. Sometimes they and their friends are mean and manipulative, and yet "those of us with disabilities never get to whine about OUR siblings nationally." Where are the *New York Times* articles about mean and manipulative siblings?

Like parents and other family members, neuro-typical siblings sometimes "say we bring things on ourselves for being 'weird,'" but it isn't "their autism" to be embarrassed or not about, Kassiane says. So lay off.

Spockette has a similar post on her Misadventures from a Different Perspective blog. She's written several posts on the difficulties of living with various members of her family, including her parents and aunt. In this post, entitled "Gah ... Family..." she writes about her sister, who's 16 and "ADD/wannabe NT."

Here Spockette tells the story of going holiday shopping with her sister. During their rounds they stop at a Wal-Mart store, where the sister (who's suffering from a case of the hives) asks Spockette to go in and buy the over-the-counter allergy medication Benadryl. But inside the crowded store Spockette experiences "sensory chaos," which causes her to forget to buy the Benadryl. When Spockette refuses to go back into the store, her sister calls her a "bitch." And then, to demonstrate how easy the task is, the sister goes in and buys the Benadryl, timing herself so as to prove her point.

Spockette describes the ensuing confrontation: "I get lectured after a look — sensitive teen doesn't want to go in to what she KNOWS is utter sensory chaos for me. Gee, thanks sis. I wasn't being a BITCH, either. I was doing my best to recover after you went in, timing yourself. Yes, that is nice that you can navigate that in eight minutes when they've moved things around again. I can't.

"Stomping on the breaks and lecturing me about 'behavior' isn't going to help when it was a 'reaction,' and not some attention-seeking, self-indulgent acting out," she writes. "Keeping oneself sane isn't a crime, last time I checked."

Call it the war of the autistic siblings. It doesn't end in childhood. On the contrary, it continues on into adulthood. And on.

As usual, I find myself in the middle. Literally. Since I get heat from both sides, from Sam and his sisters.

Well, here's my response. To siblings of autistic children or adults, I would say: stop complaining and be more supportive. Most autistic people never get the opportunity to drive, work, go to prom, travel abroad, attend their college of choice, or have a successful career. On the other hand, you have a chance to do all of these things and more. You don't have to feel guilty about your good fortune, just stop complaining. It's the least you can do to help.

And to autistic people, I would say: try not to be so demanding. Remember that you can be absolutely exasperating to live with. So be patient. It's not that your family is unwilling to help you, only that you need to give them some space so they WANT to help you. Lighten up!

Family relations. So many murky, murky issues.

Still, Cindy and I haven't changed our basic beliefs. Our philosophy remains: to each, according to his/her need. People have different needs. Some need more help and care than others. Some need different kinds of support (money, advice, information, academic assistance, whatever). The point is that everyone's different. No two children are the same. No two adults are the same. We need different things.

After the dust settled on the (once again) bruised egos of everyone involved, Cindy concluded our family discussion of sibling issues by saying to Sam's sisters, "I call this an 'ethical stance' and it's my only legacy to you, a model I hope. You have to make your own lives work, take care of others, and sustain yourself. Find relationships and good work that keep you going. And when the responsibilities fall heavily or unevenly, or when the unexpected strikes, you have to figure out a way of moving forward. That's it. That's all there is."

Amen.

Chapter 13

Communication
Corporeal and Electronic

One autistic teen in our neighborhood has a unique way of communicating. He's a good talker, a charming young man with lots of personality. But he has one little quirk: he won't talk to you unless you're in another room. So if you want to chat with this witty young man, you'll have to forget about up close and personal. Try the next room over and hope for thin walls.

The teen's inter-room conversational style works well enough at home, but not so well at school. He keeps running out of his classroom looking for an empty room. If only he could find an empty room, he could participate in class discussion. Problem is, he keeps running into rooms where other classes are in session. You can see the problem he poses for an educational system not known for its flexibility.

Sam has his own distinct and different ways of communicating, depending on his mood and the situation. If he's in a good mood, he'll employ a well-rehearsed question to strike up a conversation. For example, if he wants you to talk about the unseasonably warm weather and tornado warning we experienced on Dec. 1, 2006, he'll ask, "What happened on December 1st?" Or: "Why was December 1st so unusual?" Instead of making a statement, he wants to hear it from someone else, as a way of getting into a conversation about one of his favorite subjects. Then he'll chat fondly about that memorable event, rehashing every delicious detail. Sometimes he'll clap his hands in delight.

If he's in a bad mood, forget about even talking to him. He'll sit in a chair glaring at whoever dares comes close. If anyone in the room speaks, to him or someone else, he's say "SHHHHH!" Everyone familiar with Sam knows enough to leave him alone at that point.

Neuro-typicals often assume that autistic people, because they communicate differently, must be nonverbal and retarded. As I mentioned in an earlier chapter, the Centers for Disease Control estimate that, "About 40% of children with ASDs do not talk at all," but they fail to explain whether that number includes children who won't talk along with those who can't talk. The CDC also fails to take into account those autistic children who use facilitated and/or computer assisted communication. Consequently, the number means very little.

Like everyone else, Autistic people use body language and behaviors to communicate. When Sam barks, I know he's nervous. When he starts tapping loudly on walls, I know he wants my attention. When he races around the house, I know he's flying high and ready to go off. When he stares at me sullenly, I know he's angry or depressed. And so on. There's no failure of communication, no misunderstanding. Sam talks perfectly well, but he communicates just as effectively with his body. Sometimes more effectively.

When you live with someone, anyone, you learn to "read" that person's body; you become attuned to that person's expressions, gestures, and movements. Autistic people, I would argue, have an embodied language that's even more expressive than that of neuro-typicals. And corporeal communication can be just as effective as speech.

But the negative stereotypes persist, perpetuated (sadly) by some of the large advocacy organizations that claim to support autism. Many autistic people say that the stereotypes are more difficult to live with than autism itself. In his Pre Rain Man Autism blog, Rich Shull tells of a conversation he had with a 35-year-old autistic person in a group home. While they talked, the group home workers looked on in amazement. "His aids and home workers were STUNNED we were talking in complete thoughts!" Shull reports.

The workers had a difficult time believing their client could carry on a coherent conversation. They assumed he and his visitor were "'stupid' as we present," Shull writes. "All the autism experts in the world don't have [the] slightest clue in the world what it is we have to do to talk. If they did they would instantly realize our autism requires a bit of work but ... we can actually talk." And: "If you would simply shut up (for a start) and give us a chance to figure out a few things and quit thinking we are retarded you would be in for a pleasant shock."

The point here is that even autistic people who are perfectly capable of talking are sometimes not given the time, space, and encouragement to do so. Why? Because neuro-typicals assume that autistic people are "stupid" and unable to communicate. In addition, sometimes neuro-typicals don't hear — or don't want to hear — what autistic people are saying, especially if they are saying no to normal-ization. Neuro-typicals tend to want neuro-typical conversations. If anything out of the ordinary is said, it fails to register.

I can't count the number of times Sam has been talked down to, or talked about as though he weren't present. Sometimes people will talk to him in an insultingly loud voice, assuming he's hard of hearing or "slow." Just as bad are the people who shoot off questions staccato fashion, expecting Sam to parrot back answers. Over the years Sam has grown increasingly impatient with questions. He refuses to be interrogated. Likely as not, he'll respond, "Why do you want to know?" And if his inquisitor gets aggressive, Sam might say, "Fuck you!"

That short, succinct response has gotten Sam in a world of trouble with lots of people. But when you think about it, "Fuck you!" is a perfectly "normal" expression that one hears all the time. What other 26-year-old man, when spoken to in a harsh, conde-scending way, wouldn't respond with something similar? I hear the expression everywhere, even in my classes at the university. Young people say it all the time. It's perfectly acceptable — except, of course, when an autistic or disabled person says it, at which time lights flash, sirens blare, and neuro-typicals think: AGRESSION, HOSTILITY ... INSTITUTION!

In her Processing in Parts blog, Zilari writes about her difficulties with speech, compounded by the misconceptions of family, friends, and teachers. She remembers being "confused" by all the assumptions made about her ability to speak and by all the demands for her to respond appropriately. So much so that she began to see conversations as "a kind of puzzle or a trap" from which she had to escape.

"Despite the kinds of assumptions it might prompt, I am not going to lie and say that I can always speak, that I can always speak coherently, or that I never bang my head on walls or do anything that doesn't look 'high functioning,'" she writes. She goes on to say that she doesn't think anyone around her has any idea about the extent to which she struggles with speech, or the extent to which what comes out of her mouth is "very scripted." What she manages to say in a conversation does not always provide a true indication of what she understands or doesn't understand. Sometimes yes, sometimes no.

She comes down particularly hard on neuro-typicals who would force autistic people to speak or use other means of communication they might not be comfortable with. The choice should belong to the autistic person, guided by situation and individual preference. She explains that, for some autistic adults, speech constrains more than helps. Because of that, there is absolutely no reason why autistic people should be forced to use communication methods that don't work for them.

That is, just because an autistic person "has" speech doesn't mean the person will be able to speak in every situation. In her blog Elmindreda points out the error of dividing autistic people into speaking and non-speaking groups. The ability to speak does not necessarily — or always — imply the ability to communicate. It's common for autistic people to occasionally lose the ability to speak and/or communicate.

"Since I haven't seen a lot of descriptions of what it's actually like to lose speech, or to be able to speak but not be able to use that ability to communicate," she writes, "I will attempt to describe some of the different ways I experience those things." These events usually pass after a few minutes or hours, or when she's had a chance to rest and spend time alone, but in the meantime they can lead to potentially dangerous misunderstandings, she admits.

Her examples of "what happens on the inside" include:

- She may lose her connection to the cache of prepared sentences and sentence fragments that allow her to carry on conversations in near real-time. When this happens, she might understand things said to her, but constructing answers takes time and effort.

- She may lose the ability to improvise and modify the existing sentences and fragments according to the situation. This turns her speech into advanced echolalia, where she can give a correct response only if she happens to have it already prepared and memorized.

- She may be unable to muster the degree of muscle control necessary to get her mouth to form words properly.

- She may (because of stress, overload, or demands for rapid response) begin to confuse sentences she's prepared on her own with ones she's read by others, what she calls "topical echolalia." This can result in her saying things that are different from her actual opinions.

- She may be unable to bridge the mental chasm between her intent to say something and the act of actually starting to say it. Sometimes, no matter how hard she tries, she's unable to initiate speech, even though she may have understood everything said and know exactly what she wants to say in return.

- She may hear the words but be unable to put them into context or extract meaning from them. She can recognize each word in isolation but not together in the order in which they were spoken. They seem like a stream of random words.

- She may be too overloaded to have any means of thinking of or remembering an appropriate sentence but still be able to speak. When this happens, she usually grabs the first word or words that come to mind, resulting in a kind of "frying pan salad," often accompanied by flapping.

Reading Elmindreda's post on speech gave me a much better understanding of Sam, who in a matter of minutes can go from ebullient to unable or unwilling to speak. On a good day he's a chatterbox, with a quick wit and a wonderful sense of humor. But on the bad days, watch out. When he's overloaded and ready to go off, you can see the tension on his face. He gets confused. You can ask him what's the matter until you're blue in the face, but he can't tell you. He can't speak. He can't communicate with words. All he can do is bang his head against the wall. Only then, after he smashes his head, does he regain the ability to speak.

On other occasions Sam will have the ability to speak but not the ability to communicate with speech. He'll be talking about a neighbor, then jump to a vacation experience he had 10 years before, then to what he had for lunch yesterday, and so on. His speech follows his racing mind, wandering from one isolated, unrelated experience to another. Sometimes, when he realizes he's not being understood, he'll put his hands on his head or rest his head on the table, as though trying to refocus, to reboot. Then he'll try again.

So having the ability to speak does not necessarily mean having the ability to communicate. Likewise, not having the ability to speak does not necessarily mean not having the ability to communicate.

Non-speaking autistic children (and adults) can learn to communicate by using Facilitated Communication. With Facilitated Communication, or typing with support, an aide helps the autistic child use a keyboard, sometimes hand over hand. Critics argue that the aide, not the autistic child, is actually the one doing the communicating, but many autistic people have praised Facilitated

Communication, none more so than Sue Rubin. On the homepage of her website, she explains that for most of her childhood she was considered both autistic and retarded.

She writes: "When I was 13 years old, I was introduced to Facilitated Communication — a method of communication which allowed me to type my thoughts. With Facilitated Communication (FC), it became clear that I was not retarded, but instead, was very autistic and lacked a method of expressing myself. Sadly I was so autistic I was not aware of the world around me and looked very retarded. Using FC, I graduated from Whittier High School in Whittier, California with honors, and am now a student at Whittier College typing independently."

Like Rubin, other autistic children have started with Facilitated Communication and then progressed to computer-assisted or independent typing. Two of the most prolific autistic writers, Cal Montgomery and Amanda Baggs, use a variety of computer-assisted technologies. Montgomery writes for *Ragged Edge* magazine, and Baggs produces Ballastexistenz, possibly the most read of all autistic blogs. Because of the extraordinary richness of her blog, Baggs has become much sought after by media and medical types wanting to interview her. (See, for example, the 2007 profile of Baggs in "Living with Autism in a World Made for Others" on the CNN website.)

In one post, Baggs lists all the reasons why, when many people see her, they refuse to believe that she could have written the intellectually rigorous material on her blog. She counts the ways she's dissed, dismissed, and discounted by Neuro-typicals and their stereotypes:

She didn't write it, because someone was touching her when she "wrote" it.

She didn't write it, because she wasn't looking at the keyboard.

She didn't write it, because her speech sounds different from her writing.

She didn't write it, because she was just being exploited.

She didn't write it, because ... just *look at her!*

She didn't write it, because she can't be educated enough to write like that.

She didn't write it, because she has a mental age of 18 months.

She didn't write it, because she writes better than I can, but she's a retard.

She uses an interpreter, so the interpreter is really the person doing the talking.

Here Baggs explains that she uses a cognitive interpreter; that is, someone who understands both her body movements and her use of language. The role of the cognitive interpreter is to take a posture or a word or two and elaborate, explaining what Baggs means. If the cognitive interpreter fails to elaborate and/or translate correctly, then Baggs lets the interpreter know.

Baggs continues by saying that using a cognitive interpreter has its own problems. Often, people want to ignore her body language, even when explained by the interpreter. Another problem is the invisibility of her body language. "Because they can't see me as having body language, I am assumed to have none, and the interpreter is assumed to be pulling interpretations out of thin air," Baggs writes.

Amanda Baggs, Cal Montgomery, and Sue Rubin are living proof that electronic communication, like corporeal communication, can be just as effective as speech.

Sam communicates with speech and body language. He's never used Facilitated Communication or computer-assisted technology, but when he was an adolescent he had a word processor that he used night and day. He learned to spell and compose sentences by writing long lists of one kind or another: weather reports and houses for sale ads, mostly. He also wrote journal entries at school and Henry Huggins stories at home. At the time he loved the Henry Huggins book series for young readers, written by Beverly Cleary. When he ran out of Henry Huggins books to read, he started composing his own tales of Henry and his faithful dog, Ribsy. Today, Sam does most of his composing on e-mail. He has his own account on Yahoo, which he uses from time to time. His friends e-mail him more than he e-mails them, but that may change over time.

Like Amanda Baggs and other autistic people, Sam is often dismissed because of the way he looks. He couldn't possibly be as smart as he sounds. Must be cocktail chatter, perseverative speech, whatever. Over the years people have used different labels to dismiss Sam, all because of the way he looks. He embodies many of the familiar stereotypes that spell ABNORMAL. He's overweight and usually disheveled. He drools. He walks and sometimes dresses funny. He stares at people. He rocks his head. He barks.

Ableism runs deep in our culture. People are heavily invested in normality. Frightened by what is not normal.

Well, it's their loss, really. Such simplistic, superficial attitudes miss the wonderfully rich nuances of autistic communication in all its forms. How many times do we have to say it? Difference makes life interesting.

Take Sam, for example. Even when he uses a question to jump-start a conversation, he's not looking for a simple Q & A session. No way. He expects anecdotes and storytelling. When he asks which pizza restaurant closed downtown, he's not prompting me to say, "Uno's." He wants to hear about his favorite servers and most memorable meals. Remember Antonio, who was our server on New Years Eve 1999, the Y2K year? Remember how he danced when he brought our orders? Sam wants to hear every detail in his (or our) imaginative recreation of what was, for Sam, a magical evening.

By the time we finish collectively retelling the story of that night, we've pretty much exhausted all our jokes and tall tales. Sam loves storytelling. It's a way for him to revisit the past and reassure himself that he has a place in the world.

Chapter 14

Cognition

Sam and I like to joke with each other.

He'll walk into the room looking for a particular rap CD. I'll see him coming and say, "Let me give you one of my classical CDs."

"Me?" he'll laugh. "That would be OXYMORONIC!"

He knows full well what oxymoron means. In fact, he uses figuratively language all the time. One of the attractions of rap music is the word play: drop it like it's hot, all eaten up, shake your money-maker!

Over the years he's come up with some gems of his own. Like the time he watched a movie about a mean Russian mafia boss, conflated it with *The Wizard of Oz*, and came up with this question: "Do you believe in a broomstick God?"

Yes, Sam has come a long way from the toddler whose doctors and therapists would routinely check off his "deficits." By "deficits" they meant his autistic behaviors. They characterized his speech as perseverative and nonsensical, often marked by echolalia (that is, the stock repetition of words or phrases heard from others). They described his thought process as associational, not logical. They spoke of his inability to generalize from individual facts or bits of information. And they diagnosed Sam as lacking "Theory of Mind," meaning he did not understand that other people had independent minds, with their own thoughts, feelings, and emotions.

Probably the strangest of these pronouncements came from a genetic counselor who informed us that Sam, because of the configuration of his brain, would never be able to smell. As it turns out, Sam has an acute sense of smell!

The comments from Sam's medical team reflected the overwhelmingly negative construction of autism prevalent from the 1940s, when psychiatrist Leo Kanner of Johns Hopkins first described the disorder, through the early 1980s. It was Kanner who in a series of papers during the 1940s formulated his infamous "Refrigerator Mother" theory of autism, attributing autism to a "genuine lack of maternal warmth."

The bogus "Refrigerator Mother" theory was further popularized by psychoanalyst Bruno Bettelheim, whose 1967 book, *The Empty Fortress: Infantile Autism and the Birth of the Self,* cast a stigma over autism that still exists. Bettelheim compared autistic children to prisoners in a concentration camp, terrorized by an external world that is perceived by them to be hostile and threatening. Unfortunately, Bettelheim's "empty fortress" metaphor for autism persists to this day in the promotions and fund-raising of the large autism advocacy organizations run by non-autistics. According to these organizations, autistic people are still trapped and imprisoned by this devastating disorder. If anything, the rhetoric has become even more negative, given the urgency of the epidemic hysteria that floods these organizational websites. Reading these websites, it's hard not to come away thinking that autism has become a modern version of the Black Plague.

Well, guess what? Not only can Sam smell, he has learned to control (at least partially) his perseverative speech and echolalia. He can certainly think logically, except maybe when he's overloaded and heading for a meltdown. What's more, Sam can most definitely generalize from individual facts. In fact, Sam's psychiatrist on the adult psych ward during his last hospitalization in 2003 said Sam had "an amazing ability to conceptualize." Not a bad recommendation, coming from a psychiatrist.

As for "Theory of Mind," most recently delineated by Simon Baron-Cohen in *Mindblindness,* here's what Zilari has to say in her Processing in Parts blog. First, neuro-typicals don't have a monopoly on "Theory of the Mind." If they did, then they would be able to identify with autistic and disabled people instead of considering them somehow "subhuman."

"What most people think of as 'Theory of Mind' is really a set of shared assumptions," she writes. She goes on to say she's skeptical that anyone who doesn't consciously work at it really has a "well-developed" theory of mind. Instead, she says, people more commonly have a rather "narrow" theory of mind based on their own reactions and responses to various situations. "Obviously, if a person is a member of a cognitive/perceptual majority, it can look as if that person has some sort of uncanny ability to pick up on the emotions and motivations of others" [in the majority], she writes. However, this person's uncanny ability to pick up emotions has less to do with a highly developed theory of mind than with the attitudes and assumptions he/she shares with the majority.

Just reading or watching the nightly news, you have to wonder if anyone (or any country) has the capacity to understand that other people (or countries) have their own thoughts, feelings, and emotions, etc.

So far we've seen autism portrayed figuratively by two power-fully negative metaphors: the empty fortress, and mindblindness. Stephen Pinker adds a third nasty metaphor in his 2002 book, *The Blank Slate*. "Autism is an innate neurological condition with strong genetic roots," he writes. "Together with robots and chimpanzees, people with autism remind us that cultural learning is possible only because neurologically normal people have innate equipment to accomplish it."

Pinker adds: "A mind unequipped to discern other people's beliefs and intentions, even if it can learn in other ways, is incapable of the kind of learning that perpetuates culture."

Another autistic blogger, Larry Arnold, directly challenges Pinker's construction of autism. In one angry post in his Laurentius Rex blog, he writes: "For a professor of psychology Pinker seems extraordinarily ignorant about what language, culture and represen-tation actually are as concepts and how they relate in terms of cognition. In other words he has no idea of my world, its levels of complexity and richness. This whole network of blogs we belong to on the Autism Hub, if it proves nothing else proves that we have representation (in more [than] one sense of the word) and the means of transmitting culture[,] for if this is not it, what is?"

Good point, because the autistic bloggers associated with Autism Hub, as well as independent autistic bloggers, most definitely have a culture. And transmit culture.

Here's the point. The autistic blogosphere has a lively, intellectually stimulating culture available to anyone willing to look beyond the negative stereotypes that have been perpetuated for decades by the non-autistic autism advocacy organizations and the medical community. My advice to Pinker and Baron-Cohen and all the other autism bashers: Read Amanda Baggs, Cal Montgomery, Michele Dawson, Kassiane Montana, the Autistic Bitch from Hell, and all the other bloggers, and then tell me autistic people are incapable of culture.

Don't misunderstand. I'm not downplaying the difficulties many autistic people have with communication and cognition. After all, autistic people freely admit to having a different cognitive process; that's what neurodiversity is all about. But it's one thing to say autistic people have different neurological wiring, and something else entirely to say they are incapable of culture, abstract thinking, or whatever.

Still on this subject, Larry Arnold adds the following: "What autism is to me is a set of differences, probably neuro biological that govern the way we interpret the social, perceptual and sensory world. We are born with a different programme [sic]."

So, if autistic people are born with a different neurological "program," then how do we describe that program? Some autistic people claim to be visual thinkers; that is, they think with images instead of words. Probably the most prominent writer among these visual thinkers is Temple Grandin. She begins her book, *Thinking in Pictures*, with this statement: "I think in pictures. Words are like a second language to me. I translate both spoken and written words into full-color movies, complete with sound, which run like a VCR tape in my head. When somebody speaks to me, his words are instantly translated into pictures."

Grandin argues that most autistic people tend to have a strong visual orientation. "One of the most profound mysteries of autism has been the remarkable ability of most autistic people to excel at visual spatial skills while performing so poorly at verbal skills," she writes. She claims to have a "video library in my imagination" where she stores information as images in her memory. A particular image will trigger, by association, a particular memory or concept.

"Unlike those most people, my thoughts move from video-like, specific images to generalizations and concepts," Grandin writes. "Growing up, I learned to convert abstract ideas into pictures as a way to understand them. I visualized concepts such as peace or honesty with symbolic images. I thought of peace as a dove, an Indian peace pipe, or TV newsreel footage of the signing of a peace agreement. Honesty was represented by an image of placing one's hand on the Bible in court."

Rich Shull is another autistic writer who calls himself a "proficient picture thinker." In his Pre Rain Man Autism blog, Shull describes how his mind works, converting images to words so that he can speak. His mind functions like a computer software program that converts one language to another. He comments on the frustration he felt growing up when he couldn't convert images to words fast enough to please family, friends, and teachers. Because of his frustration, he sometimes experienced dyslexia and stuttering.

Shull provides a fascinating description of the thought process of a visual thinker. As a way of fitting in, he tried to streamline his brain-generated images so as to keep up with traditional thought patterns. He compares the process to pushing the fast forward button on a tape recorder. Sometimes, if his picture thoughts were not fully developed and translated correctly and he tried to speak, he came off as being "very dyslexic."

"Stuttering seems to be kind of verbal version of dyslexia," he writes. He explains that if he has several completed picture thoughts that all can be converted to words to be spoken, he can stutter for hours trying to discover which picture thought to use. Once he decides on which picture thought to translate to words, the stuttering stops and he can talk again.

Similar to Grandin, Shull claims to have observed a pattern among autistic people from around the world: "we seem to share the common Autism thought process ... and our picture thoughts seem to be the same even if the language we speak is different."

I've asked Sam on many occasions whether he thinks in pictures or words. Inevitably, he's offended. "What do you mean?" he'll say. "Of course I think in words."

But I'm not so sure that's entirely true. When Sam was a toddler, he would differentiate sounds by colors. He'd say, that's a blue sound, or that's a red sound. For him sounds had a visual component. And words? Hard to say at this late date, since as soon as he entered school he was discouraged from this line of visual thinking by teachers and counselors. Now if you ask him about sounds having colors, he gets embarrassed and refuses to answer.

Sometimes, though, when he's trying to express a difficult thought, he'll start to stutter and his hands will shake violently, as though he's trying to jump-start the process of converting images into words.

I'm certain of one thing, though. Sam thinks in metaphors. That's why he's so drawn to the word-play of rap music. Bust a move! Drop it like it's hot! When he misspeaks, he might say, "That's a malfunction." Or, "Let me reboot and try again." When he wants to go shopping at Kroger, he might say, "I need some Krogerian Therapy."

When Sam identifies a person with a certain trait, he takes that person's name and makes a verb out of the name. For example, if someone named Mitch Firestone is always late or never shows up, Sam will transform Firestone into a verb and come up with: "He Firestoned me." Meaning, of course, that he (whoever he is) was either late or didn't show at all.

To Sam, "Doing a Charlie" means walking out on your wife (long story there, concerning his younger sister's ex-husband).

"Doing a Julie" means to take a few tokes (no explanation needed). And so on.

Sam has an entire book of metaphors to describe tornado clouds, much as Eskimos have multiple words to describe snow. His current favorite is "broomstick cloud."

Why metaphors? I suppose comparing one thing to another is a way of making the unfamiliar, familiar. And also a way of generalizing. For example, by using the expression "broomstick cloud," he connects tornado (a natural phenomenon) to evil witch (a mythical creature) to malevolent force or God (an abstraction).

Not bad for one short expression.

Obviously, different autistic people write about their cognitive process in different ways. In her The Art of Understanding blog, Chasmatazz distinguishes "linear" from "holistic" thought and suggests that autistic people are more likely to be holistic thinkers. By linear thinker, she means "someone with a tendency to consider things separately, to note differences, to divide and sub-divide, to analyze, to discriminate." She argues that from linear thought arose the concepts of number, sequence, hierarchy, definition, boundary, ownership, competition, and so on.

On the other hand, holistic thinkers tend to "think in wholes, to see similarities, make connections, group together." With holistic thinkers, you might expect difficulty with language, since language is thought broken down into parts. You might also expect holistic thinkers to have difficulty with processing separate stimuli. Chasmatazz continues: "You might expect difficulty with limits and boundaries. You might expect 'picture thought'—a tendency to conceive of broad, complex understandings as single 'big pictures,' not necessarily visual. You might even expect a fascination with parts of objects, since parts are foreign. In short, you might expect to see something which closely resembles what we now call autism."

Now I certainly don't believe all autistic people are holistic thinkers (or visual thinkers, for that matter), but I find the connection interesting because it helps explain why and how Sam uses metaphors. That is, "to conceive of broad, complex understandings as single 'big pictures'"—or in Sam's case, metaphors. You could argue, I suppose, that metaphors are a manifestation of holistic thinking.

For Sam, metaphors are a way of making broad connections. A way of making his life, which sometimes feels hopelessly fragmented, whole.

I would never claim to fully understand Sam's cognitive process (or that of anyone else, autistic or non-autistic, for that matter). But I do know a few things. Sam is not an empty fortress. He doesn't suffer from mindblindness. And he's not a blank slate.

He's just Sam, with his own thoughts, feelings, and emotions. His own agenda. His own life.

By way of conclusion, let me quote Interverbal from his blog of the same name. Here are the first three lines of his sonnet, "Shall I compare thee to a norm referenced score?" I dedicate my re-use of the poem to Leo Kanner, Bruno Bettelheim, Simon Baron-Cohen, and Stephen Pinker:

> Shall I compare thee to a norm referenced score?
> Thou might just be two deviations from the mean.
> Rough charting makes it hard to know for sure.

Chapter 15

Agoraphobia, or Don't Call Us...

Socially, Sam is a chameleon.

One day he's hyper-social, eager to chat with everyone, friend or foe.

The next day he's overcome by agoraphobia, paranoid and fearful of everyone he encounters. Sometimes the swing can occur in a matter of hours.

When he's in a friendly mood, feeling frisky, he'll joke about his anti-social self, his Jack Burns as he calls it. Jack Burns, you might remember, is the character Robert DeNiro plays in the Focker movies. Suspicious of everyone, especially Greg Focker (who he's convinced is a pothead, or worse), Burns resorts to polygraph tests and injections of truth serum, while constantly saying, "I'm watching you!"

Funny to laugh about it afterward, but not so funny when Jack is back.

By way of illustration, let me tell you about the last (as in VERY last) party we held at our house. Wanting to celebrate the end of the school year, we invited both students and faculty. We scheduled the gathering from 4:30 to 7:30 P.M. on a Friday afternoon, because Sam goes out with one of his buddies every Friday from 4:30 to about 7 P.M. Knowing Sam's penchant for disruptive behavior if the mood so strikes, we wanted to minimize the risk as much as possible. We figured the guests would begin leaving shortly after Sam returned, so even if he came back home in an unsocial mood we could probably avoid a meltdown. Our bad.

On the day of the party we felt cautiously optimistic when Sam popped out of bed in a bright, cheerful mood. He left with his friend shortly after 4:30, with rap music blaring on the car radio, as per. Our guests began arriving as Sam and his companion drove off down the street toward his favorite pizzeria. The weather was perfect for an outdoor gathering. So far, so good.

So the party gets rolling. The guests congregate on the back deck, enjoying drinks and a potluck dinner. Everyone's exhausted from the long academic year. They can't get enough to eat or drink. Kids swim in the pool, while their parents watch from nearby chaises. The patio tables are crowded with students and faculty talking shop, sharing stories about their classes and their teaching. No one seems to have a care in the world.

Except us. We're worried about Sam, worried about what he'll say and do when he walks in and sees all the people, most of them strangers.

Come 7 P.M., none of the guests have left. Our anxiety level ratchets up another notch.

Then in walks Sam. One look at his face and it's clear that he's not a happy camper. "Who are you?" he asks the first person he sees. "Who are you?" he asks the next person. And so on down the line.

"Hey Sam, come join us," I say from a nearby table, trying to include him in our conversation.

Someone leaves to make room for him at the table, happy to get away from the nervous vibes emanating from Sam's body.

"Hi Sam!" everyone says at once. All our friends and acquaintances know of Sam.

"Who are you?"

They introduce themselves one at a time.

Sam continues to pepper them with questions. He won't respond when someone asks him a question, won't join a conversation. Instead, he rattles off one hostile question after another.

He's working himself into a frenzy, a time bomb waiting to go off.

Now, finally, some of our guests start to leave.

131

Trying to defuse the situation, I move into the kitchen and start clearing some of the dirty dishes. Sometimes if I can get him away from the stressor, back to his usual routine, I can help him calm down. He follows me inside, but when I ask if he wants to go down to his pad and use the bathroom, watch a DVD, or whatever, he just glares at me. Nice try.

Sam can't separate himself. He can't just walk away. Instead, he goes back outside. "When are you leaving?" he starts asking everyone. Most of the faculty have gone by now, but some of the students have decided to stick it out to the bitter end. I do mean bitter.

Now Cindy tries to divert his attention. "Sam, come over and talk to John."

Sam likes John, so he follows his mom down to the pool and has a brief conversation with John, who's trying his best to engage Sam. They're old friends.

But Sam can't stop the train that's about to derail.

He heads back to the kitchen, then starts to hit Cindy when she tries to get his attention.

"Sam, PLEASE, come inside!" I plead with him.

He steps inside, then shouts, "NO! NO!"

Suddenly he lurches forward, knocking down the screen door, then bangs his head against the door jam.

"Whoop, time for everyone to go," Cindy says matter-of-factly, almost cheerfully, making the best of an awkward situation.

"Yep. Not to worry. Just Sam being Sam," I say. Making a joke is better than apologizing. I'm beyond apologizing for Sam's behavior. People either understand or they don't.

By now the stragglers are grabbing towels and food containers and heading for the exits faster than if someone had yelled 'fire' in a crowded theater. Some don't even bother to say goodbye, they just go, running for their cars. Running for cover.

No one can break up a party faster than Sam. Last call takes on new meaning when he's in one of his anti-social moods.

Only when he sees them leaving does Sam start to relax. He

moves away from the door and follows me down to his pad, where we go through our usual routine. I give him a warm bath and wash away the blood (not much tonight, thankfully). Then he gets into his pajamas and turns on the Weather Channel, relaxing in front of the TV until bedtime.

By the time we finish the dishes he's humming happily down in the Yellow Submarine, engaged in his usual activities.

I wait until he goes to bed, then reattach and repair the screen door as much as I can in the dark. The metal frame is bent and the screen punched out, but it'll hold until tomorrow afternoon, when I'll buy another one at Lowe's or Home Depot.

Just another routine Sam repair. Standard home maintenance.

So what gives? Why does he fall into these anti-social moods?

Sam won't talk about it, of course. What else is new?

"Just my impulses," is all he'll ever say.

From what I read in the autistic blogosphere, people problems aren't that unusual. Many of the bloggers write about being self-conscious and having low self-image, being made to feel bad about how they look and behave, which only makes them look and behave even more badly (that is, atypically). Most neuro-typicals don't understand the power of negative stereotypes or just how corrosive the stigma attached to disability can be for disabled people. Having to live under the normative gaze can be more difficult than living with a disability.

Amanda Baggs writes in her Ballastexistenz blog that the reason she feels self-conscious isn't because there's anything inherently shameful about being autistic, but because she and other autistic people have been taught to feel shame and embarrassment for being defective and/or inferior. At times feeling self-conscious has made her want to disappear. "I can remember hiding in closets and being accused of trying to make people find me, and running away from people only to be accused of trying to make people chase after me," she writes.

Another blogger, Lori Berkowitz, addresses this same issue. "Sometimes, I really hate being me." she writes in her LBnuke blog.

"I get very down on myself and very jealous of other people. I get tired of having a hard time doing basic things like reading, traveling, talking, leaving the house, working, even playing video games! It makes me feel like an idiot."

Like Baggs and Berkowitz, Sam is acutely aware of how he looks to other people. He suffers painfully from low self-image. He sees himself through the negative reactions of others. When he's feeling bad about himself, he doesn't want to be around other people, especially strangers. He wants to hang with his parents or one of his other companions, tell some jokes and chill. That is, he wants to surround himself with the familiar and the comfortable.

I know all this, and yet it doesn't make it any easier to accept not having a social life. I remember hearing an anecdote not long ago. The wife and caregiver of a man with Alzheimer's was talking about social death. You don't get invited back to parties, she said, after your husband drops his pants and urinates in the punch bowl! Welcome to my world.

So I don't want to make excuses for Sam and say everything's okay, because it's not. Who doesn't want comfort? Who isn't self-conscious?

And anyway, Sam's agoraphobia isn't always caused by low self-esteem. He's done the same thing in small groups of friends, people who have known and cared about him for years. No, it's more about wanting to be the center of attention. And about control. He wants to be the center of attention and to control the social interaction around him. That's why he prefers a one-on-one situation, where he's only manipulating one other person. Just being with more than one person at a time stresses Sam, sometimes to the breaking point.

On top of all that, sometimes Sam struggles with paranoia. He'll worry that people are talking about him or plotting against him. Or he'll worry that people are making fun of him. For example, if I make a joke about his rap music, he might come back with, "Are you making fun of me?"

He's especially touchy about the way he looks and dresses, as well as the way he eats. When he eats, he's often a bit messy. But if you make a comment or ask him to clean up, watch out. He thinks you're making fun of him.

But hold on. It gets worse.

Issues of attention, control, and paranoia all coalesce (like the perfect storm) around one seemingly innocuous household electronic. The telephone. Yes, the telephone has become Sam's primary trigger. If he's feeling anti-social and paranoid, the ring of a telephone can send him off the deep end.

Why the telephone? I think, originally, it had to do with teachers and aides calling from school to convey the litany of Sam's misbehaviors. The reports, like the news, were always bad.

Today Sam's telephone phobia combines both control issues and paranoia. He wants to control who we talk with and what plans we make.

Sam has super-sensitive hearing, so even though we turn the ringer down to its lowest level, he hears it anyway and comes running up from his pad demanding, "Who's on the phone? Who's on the phone?"

If the call concerns him, especially if it's from a doctor's office or the MRDD, he might try to grab the phone out of my hand or push the off button. He's been known to pull the telephone cord out of the wall jack.

Even calls from Sam's two older sisters can upset him. He's keenly jealous of them, I guess because they live full, independent lives. Sometimes he'll talk to them, but most of the time not.

But hold on. It gets much worse.

To complicate matters, as if they weren't complicated enough, Sam remembers when we've had to call 911 and ask for help. Those events remain vivid in his memory, just below the surface during each and every transaction with the telephone. The three separate occasions have merged into one grand assault on his identity, magnified by his imagination. He knows the routine. We make the call, the police arrive, and he ends up on the psych ward.

Now, whenever Sam becomes aggressive, he'll ask if we're going to call the police. "Are you going to make the call?" he'll ask, fearfully.

So if Sam thinks we're about to make the call, he'll rush to one phone after another and try to destroy them all. First he'll smash the receivers and then douse them with water in the hall bathroom. Sometimes he'll take the wet receivers outside and toss them on the front deck. More often, though, he'll simply drop the offending devices in the toilet. Water ruins the batteries and makes the phones unusable. We can't make the call if none of the phones work. Or so he thinks.

Over the last several years I've fished at least a dozen receivers out of the toilet. Not something you like to freely admit, even if it is the absolute, absurd truth. Absurdity will set you free? I don't think so.

At one point Sam's fear got so bad he smashed and doused his own phone, the one we installed in the kitchen of the Yellow Submarine so that he could call his friends in private. I found the phone in his toilet one day when I came down to clean his pad. It was as though he was afraid of himself, afraid HE would make the call! That's the level of his fear: visceral, instinctual, beyond reason and rationality.

The first time I called the police, Sam was waiting out on the front deck, among the fragments of our late cordless phone. I was standing on the lawn, safely out of range. When the officers arrived, they made their way slowly toward Sam and, after a few minutes, managed to talk him down. Sam cooperated and agreed to go with them to Children's Hospital.

"Will you follow us down to Children's?" the oldest of the two officers asked me.

"Yeah — just let me call my wife," I said, getting down on my hands and knees.

Sam and the officers watched incredulously as I rummaged through the fragments of phone scattered on the deck.

"Nope ... okay," I said, still on all fours. "Let me check the phone that's in the toilet."

"Pardon?"

"The one in the toilet."

The officer looked confused. "Tell you what; we'll meet you down there," he said, eager to be gone.

Shortly after this incident we purchased our first cell phones, which we keep with us at all times. So far Sam hasn't tried to destroy the cell phones. Out of sight, out of mind, I suppose.

We still keep one cordless phone in the house, just so Sam can call his friends when he's feeling social. Which, to be fair, is most of the time.

But unless I'm expecting a doctor's call, I won't go near the cordless phone. No, thank you. Instead, I make all my calls from my office or from my cell phone. As far away from Sam as I can possibly get.

Chapter 16

Too Crazy for the Psych Ward?

I called Sam's mom to tell her the news: our son had been kicked off the psych ward for being too crazy.

"How is that possible? How can you be too crazy for the psych ward?"

Good question.

So I described the ward psychiatrist, a tiny wisp of a man from Sri Lanka who moved in silence from room to room as though not wanting to disturb his patients. Whenever someone asked him a question, a pained expression fell across his face. The curtain of pain, I described it. Every time he entered the seclusion room to see Sam, he would unlock the door and creep stealthily into the room until Sam moved toward him. "Saaaaam," he would say in a surprisingly deep voice, creeping backwards out of the room and deftly clicking the door shut behind him. Like a bullfighter wielding a door instead of a cape.

"Curtain of pain?" Cindy asked, confused by my oblique explanation. When push comes to shove I tend to be a prevaricator; Cindy takes action.

"I'm on my way."

We'd made a big mistake the night before, when Sam had spun out of control and started pushing and punching. His private psychiatrist had been changing his meds, trying to find the right mood stabilizer, which probably contributed to the meltdown. We needed intervention fast, so we called 911 and asked for help. The township police arrived quickly and prevented Sam from hurting us or doing any more damage to the house. Now the question was what to do with him until he calmed down. At 22, he was too old for the adolescent psych ward at Children's Hospital. Instead of going down to the inner-city university hospital, we opted for the local community hospital, which was much closer and more convenient for everyone. Our bad, it turned out.

When Cindy arrived, we did our best to provide a united front in our conversation with the psychiatrist. Sam needed to be on a psych ward. To verify that, he only had to read last night's notes from the emergency room. Or ask the Emergency Room nurses, who'd taken their share of abuse.

A quiet, gentle man, the psychiatrist made a clicking noise with his tongue as he looked through Sam's chart. "Twenty-two-year-old ... Caucasian ... male ... Hydrocephalus ... Autism Spectrum Disorder ... Mood Disorder," his voice growing more somber with each new diagnosis. Finally he threw up his hands. "What's to be done?"

Exactly. What's to be done?

He went on to explain that they had nothing to offer, no room at the inn. They didn't treat people like Sam. Most of their patients suffered from depression or anxiety. "Maybe anorexia, but nothing like this," he said sadly, the curtain of pain descending over his face.

And he was right about his hospital not treating Sam. They kept him locked in the isolation room, entering only to bring him meds and food. Otherwise they stayed away, offering no therapy or activities, nothing but a hospital gurney in a barren room, its walls stained by blood where Sam had banged his head. Incarceration, without any pretense of treatment.

I nodded to Cindy.

She nodded back.

"NOT autism," he said, as if to clarify what he'd just said.

To be fair, this psych ward was in a midsize community hospital unused to treating patients who were loud and intimidating and perfectly capable of doing just about anything, including head-banging. Here, they saw their role as norming; that is, getting their

139

depressed and anxious suburban patients back to their normal routines as quickly as possible. Normality, that was their goal. So you can see the problem. Even on his best behavior, Sam didn't exactly fit their definition of "normal."

So that brought us to plan B.

What was plan B?

"Weeeeell ... we could probate him to the state institution in Columbus." He could tell by our expressions that sending Sam to the state institution in Columbus was a nonstarter. "Or, we could transfer him to the psych ward at the university hospital. It says here that your son sees a psychiatrist at the university who prescribes his medication. That might be the best course of action."

He assured us he was only thinking about what was best for Sam. Yeah, right.

So Cindy called our son's psychiatrist, who did indeed work at the university medical center and did indeed prescribe Sam's meds, after the bi-monthly 10-minute office visit and $145 bill.

I could tell by the rising volume of Cindy's voice that Sam's psychiatrist was not buying plan B. Number one, she didn't admit or see patients in-hospital. Number two, the psych ward at the university hospital did not routinely accept people with autism. At which point Cindy yelled into the phone and informed her that she had a responsibility to her patient, that it was unethical to do nothing and say it wasn't her problem.

"I am NOT unethical!" came hissing through the phone loud enough for me to hear.

Eventually the shouting devolved into a quieter exchange. Then Cindy passed the phone to the ward psychiatrist, and when I saw him smile I knew that Sam was on his way to the medical center. Bye-bye Sam.

Later that night we followed the ambulance transferring Sam to the university hospital. He arrived in restraints, which the aides decided to keep on overnight since the accompanying paperwork described Sam as "extremely violent."

So I was surprised when I arrived the following morning to find

Sam sitting in his room, without restraints, chatting with the nurses. "He's fine," one nurse laughed. "We've been talking about Uno's pizza."

"She likes it as much as I do!" Sam said gleefully. I hadn't seen him smile or laugh for several days.

Why the change?

I began to understand why when the psychiatrist who happened to be on duty came into the room to meet Sam. Disliking shrinks, Sam did his usual number, moving ominously toward the man with his arms outstretched. His Frankenstein routine. But this psychiatrist didn't flinch; he stood up, his six-foot, six-inch frame towering a foot above Sam. "We don't fight here, Sam," he said firmly, taking hold of Sam's arms. "We solve problems."

Sam returned to his chair.

As simple as that. Or maybe not so simple.

Here's the thing. Sam had been fearful of being sent away to a "lockdown ward" since one of his doctors, a neurologist, told him years ago that he would be sent away to an institution if he couldn't stop hitting other people. Thank you, doctor. Predictably, Sam immediately started hitting me and anyone else in range while the good doctor hurried off to work more wonders with other patients.

Since then, Sam panics when he thinks we might send him away. We won't, of course; in fact, we've insisted that Sam not be institutionalized or put in a traditional group home. Sam knows that, but he forgets in the heat of the moment on a bad day when he's had trouble controlling his aggressive behaviors. Even worse are the really bad days, when we've had to call 911 and ask for assistance. When the police cruiser pulls up in front of the house, Sam doesn't have the presence of mind to step back and reason with himself that his parents would not send him away to an institution.

So Sam panics. He reacts with a visceral, fiercely physical fear. His first stay on a "lockdown ward," the adolescent psych unit at Children's, only made matters worse. So, too, did his experience at the small community hospital, because there the nervous psychiatrist and his equally nervous aides were afraid to get near Sam. Their meek, tentative behavior sent the message that he was a wild man out of control, that he was dangerous, someone to be feared. Whenever they dared approach, Sam could see a look of terror in their eyes. And their fear, reflected back, made Sam feel even more afraid. Of himself.

Not surprisingly, Sam's fear of being locked up echoes throughout the autistic blogosphere. Institutionalization, like no other issue, unites autistic bloggers in their condemnation of parents, doctors, social workers, and other professionals who would institutionalize autistic people. No one speaks more forcefully about this issue than people who have been institutionalized at certain periods in their lives. Two of the most eloquent autistic writers who speak from personal experience are Amanda Baggs and Cal Montgomery.

Here's Baggs writing about her fear: "I fear being put in an institution, of any kind, whether a large institution, a group home, a nursing home, or a psychiatric ward." She lists some of her more pressing fears: that she will be abandoned, that she will be denied medical care, and that she will not be given a workable communication system. Even more frightening, she fears people might decide to kill her in order to spare her the unendurable suffering they imagine she's experiencing. "I fear being treated as a non-person," she writes.

Cal Montgomery has written about her own experience of incarceration. In "Critic of the Dawn," a review essay for *Ragged Edge* magazine, Montgomery chastises her parents for pressuring her to accept institutionalization (as opposed to guardianship). Her memories of the institution include "the agitated stupor of drugs, the unrelenting pain of electroshock, the degradation of smiling 'yes' while being told my every experience was wrong."

"And I remember the times I could not speak and had no keyboard," she writes, "the times I slammed my head against a wall over and over until the staff looked for a helmet I couldn't remove, and I am sadly grateful that they haven't known a world in which communication and self-respect are possible only with blood and broken bones."

Thankfully, none of Sam's experiences have been as negative as

Montgomery's. In fact, his stay at the university hospital turned out to be positive. Why? Partly because Sam felt more comfortable on a ward where the staff wasn't afraid of him; they didn't react to him as though he were a dangerous criminal. On the contrary. They conveyed the quiet, calming message that he was in a safe place where he could work on solving his problems. That is, instead of putting him in restraints or isolation, they spent time with him, really listening to what he had to say.

Equally important, the university hospital was located in the inner city and served a diverse clientele. Here, instead of depressed, anxious suburbanites, Sam found a ward filled with marginalized, cast-off people who fell through the cracks of normality. The staff was accustomed to dealing with patients who were different — and challenging. They didn't bombard Sam with rules, regulations, and schedules. If Sam wanted to participate in activities or talk with staff, he could. Or he could stay in his room. The choice was his to make.

I don't want to make the experience seem overly rosy. It was still a psych ward, not a resort. But a brief stay on a psych ward is not the same thing as an extended stay in a long-term institution. I'll have to disagree with Amanda Baggs on this point.

Fact is, at the university hospital Sam began to lose his fear of the "lockdown ward." His sea-change didn't happen all at once, of course. It took place gradually, over the course of a week. Lots of people helped make his stay positive, beginning with the intake nurse who became Sam's favorite confidant and Uno's co-enabler.

Other people were equally important. Let's just say that Sam wasn't the only gangsta rapper on the ward! He developed a friendship with an older patient and rap aficionado who liked to walk up and down the hallway. Sam would be standing just inside the door to his room listening to music when his friend would come bopping down the hallway. "Wassup?" Sam would ask.

"Wass-down?" his friend would reply, making both of them laugh.

Then there was the ward psychiatrist who was assigned to Sam, a striking and intensely intellectual young man who seemed to have a genuine interest in his patients. Dr. B., as Sam called him, showed an amazing ability to get Sam to talk. Every other psychiatrist, psychologist, therapist, and counselor we'd taken Sam to see over the years had basically given up and admitted defeat. Instead of offering therapy, they allowed Sam to talk about whatever he wanted to talk about, usually weather. Not Dr. B. He managed to engage Sam in conversation about the big stuff, the things that mattered most to Sam. Like learning to control his aggressive behaviors. Like getting along with other people.

Sam responded to him, I think, because Dr. B. took him seriously. Instead of the usual patronizing small talk that Sam had grown accustomed to, Dr. B. actually talked to him about his behavior problems and listened to what Sam had to say about himself, what he wanted, what he needed.

Being taken seriously provided a big boost to Sam's self-esteem, which he desperately needed.

And Sam took great comfort in Dr. B. telling him not to feel badly about being hospitalized for only the second time in 22 years.

"What if I have more problems?" Sam asked, knowing full well that his problems weren't about to magically disappear.

"You can always come back if you need help," Dr. B. said, explaining that the hospital offered a psychiatric emergency room where, if people are upset, they can come in to talk with social workers and counselors and stay until they calm down. "Sometimes just talking with someone other than your parents can help people work out their problems."

Sam liked the idea of a safe haven. He felt reassured. No longer did he have to be afraid of himself—he could get help.

Later that week, at the discharge meeting, Dr. B. again praised Sam. "He has an amazing ability to conceptualize," he said, describing some of the conversations he'd had with Sam.

On the way back to the ward Dr. B. stopped me in the hall. "Don't feel like it's a defeat if Sam has to come in again," he said. "This is only his second hospitalization. That's nothing. Believe me, we have a lot of frequent fliers here."

I thanked him for being so good with Sam. He was the only psychiatrist or psychologist who'd ever really talked with Sam. The others had just made small talk and prescribed drugs. I told him all that.

He nodded, lingering in the hallway. He seemed to want to talk.

"Actually, I want to thank YOU," he said, pausing. "Thank you for coming in every day ... and for the way you are with Sam."

I was surprised, to say the least, that our conversation had taken this turn. I didn't know what to say.

"What I mean is the way you treat Sam ... and others ... people who society doesn't always value," he said, choosing his words carefully. "I've learned a lot from watching you and Sam. I just wanted you to know that."

Now I was truly shocked. What I was hearing was a disability rights perspective. Was Dr. B. a disability activist? It seemed far-fetched until he continued.

"I have a daughter with Down Syndrome."

Now it all made sense. People who hold enlightened views on disability almost always have experienced disability. Without a direct connection, people just don't understand.

We stood there in the hallway, two fathers talking about our children. Without exception, it was the most amazing conversation I've ever had with a psychiatrist. Or any doctor, for that matter.

Four years later Sam had his third and last (to date) visit to a psych facility, when the police dropped him off at the university hospital's psychiatric emergency room for an overnight chill-out. Once again, he'd become self-destructive and aggressive, hitting me and smashing things around the house. But this time he'd calmed down by the time the police arrived. He chatted with them, then climbed into the cruiser for the ride downtown. "Dr. B. said I could come back if I needed to," he said.

When I picked him up next morning, Sam was proud that he hadn't hurt anyone in the ER. In fact, he was apologetic and repentant, promising that he would never again break anything around the house or hurt me.

I'd heard it all before.

But still, compared to his first two visits to the psych ward, this was nothing. A sleepover. He wasn't even admitted to the hospital. Just being there reminded him of what he needed to do — and he did it.

On the way home I thought of Dr. B. He was right, of course; I shouldn't feel defeated if I had to bring Sam back to the university hospital. If Sam needed help, then he needed help. If he needed to be in a safe, quiet place, then that's where he needed to be until he regained control.

Did three visits to the psych ward in eight years make Sam a frequent flyer? I knew Dr. B. wouldn't think so, and because of him, I didn't either.

Chapter 17

Medicalization

Disability activists commonly reject what they call the "medical model" of disability. The medical model pathologizes disability as individual defect to be corrected or eliminated by medical science. That is, disabled people possess defective bodies and/or minds that require medical intervention in order to be made functional, or "normal." The medical model privileges doctors and other medical professionals to speak for and on behalf of their disabled patients, who become medical objects. As a consequence, disabled people are diagnosed, labeled, defined, treated, and controlled by an all-powerful medical establishment.

Instead, disability activists generally advocate the "social model" of disability. That is, they read disability as partly (if not primarily) socially constructed. They argue that disabled people are limited less by their actual impairments (visual, hearing, mobility, etc.) than by the lack of accommodations provided by their social environment, as well as by the disabling attitudes and assumptions of an "ableist" society. Instead of medicalization, the social model of disability promotes inclusion, accessibility, and accommodation. In addition, activists insist that disabled people speak for and define themselves.

The classic example of how the social model works goes something like this. Say a disabled woman who uses a wheelchair is prevented from voting at her neighborhood polling station because of a lack of curb cut-outs and/or ramps. Is she politically disenfranchised by her mobility impairment, or by the lack of access provided by her social environment?

Here's a real example involving a young man with an Autism Spectrum Disorder from Sam's social club (of Hooters fame). Andy also had a seizure disorder, ordinarily controlled by medication. Well, one day Andy had a seizure at work and was promptly fired from his clerical job. His employer fired him not because of his job performance, which was satisfactory, but because co-workers couldn't "deal" with his seizures, however rare. So here's the question: did Andy lose his job because of his impairment (his seizure disorder) or because of his unaccommodating social environment (the stigma attached to epilepsy and the lack of understanding and accommodation at his office)?

Sadly, Andy had lost several other jobs for much the same reason. This time, though, he opted for experimental surgery designed to eliminate his seizure disorder altogether. To make a long story short, the experimental surgery proved disastrous. Andy spent weeks in a coma, months in a long-term rehabilitation hospital, and today is still not fully ambulatory or able to communicate as well as before the surgery. Ironically, the attempt to eliminate his "individual defect" only worsened his impairment — and his disability.

So how might have a more enlightened model of disability prevented this disaster? First, Andy's doctors and employers might have focused less on his impairment and more on his disability. Their discussions might have addressed the social situation at Andy's workplace: the lack of understanding and accommodation, and the fear of disability. Such negotiations might have resulted in a radically different course of action (and a radically different outcome). Instead of experimental surgery to eliminate the seizure disorder, an attempt might have been made to enlist a nurse or social worker to educate his co-workers about seizures. Such basic knowledge would have gone a long way toward defusing the stigma attached to this disorder, thus promoting the accommodations necessary for Andy to remain a productive worker.

The medical model versus the social model.

We're seeing the same argument play out now in the autism wars. On one side are the large advocacy organizations run by non-autistics (such as Autism Speaks, Cure Autism Now, and Autism Society of America) arguing that autism is a "devastating" disease of epidemic proportions that desperately needs to be cured. Arrayed against the "curebie" establishment are autistic-run advocacy organizations (such as Autism Network International), as well as individual autistic activists and bloggers, who argue that autism is a manifestation of neurodiversity and needs to be understood and accommodated, not cured.

As we saw in an earlier chapter, autistic bloggers tend to dismiss all talk of an autism epidemic as hype. With some notable exceptions, such as Sue Rubin, they support the social theory of disability in general and the neurodiversity theory of autism in particular. In her blog Chasmatazz writes about her gradual conversion to the social model. She admits that it took her a long time to "own" the term disabled, because the only definition for the term she knew was the medical one, which she rejected. She explains: "I knew that my differences were not flaws ... and any difficulty I encountered was dependent on a social environmental context. Without realizing it, I had owned the social model of disability."

She points out that most non-disabled people take for granted their functionality, not realizing the wealth of accommodations they enjoy or the extent to which they are dependent on society (and the extent to which they would be disabled without those accommodations). "Many disabled people present a different set of needs than the majority, and therefore require different accommodations, but those accommodations afford no more than equal access, equal status, and equal protection," she writes.

Or consider Zilari in this post from her Processing in Parts blog. She confesses to having a much more "serious" mindset than when she first began writing her blog, explaining, "This comes, in part, from realizing how lucky I am to never have been institutionalized." She points out that once you've been classified as "abnormal," people treat you very differently and interpret all your actions through a "frighteningly medicalized filter."

Why does Zilari say "frighteningly" medicalized filter? To begin to understand why, take a look at some of the latest (as of this writing) and hottest autism research to hit the broadcast and print media. This study reports on genomic research linking particular genes to an increased risk of autism. The original research article, published in the journal *Science*, begins with this paragraph:

> Autism spectrum disorders (ASDs) ... are characterized by language impairments, social deficits, and repetitive behaviors. The onset of symptoms occurs by the age of 3 and usually requires extensive support for the lifetime of the afflicted. The prevalence of ASD is estimated to be 1 in 166, making it a major burden to society.

Here we see the medical model at work. Differences become "deficits." Autistic people become "the afflicted," a term ripe with negative connotations, especially in the biblical rhetoric of the Old and New Testaments. The *Oxford English Dictionary* defines afflicted as "Cast down, depressed, oppressed in mind, body, or estate; hence, grievously troubled or distressed." As I have written elsewhere: "The afflicted are cast down by God either as punishment for their sins or as a test to verify their faith. Thus the disabled, seen as deformed in both body and spirit, are thought to be literal manifestations of God's displeasure and/or wrath."

But the nastiest part of this construction of autism comes at the very end, when autistic people are designated a "major burden to society." By using this kind of hype, as they routinely do, scientists, science writers, and science journalists participate in stigmatizing autistic people. We see this social burden rhetoric applied to other groups of people as well, including (in recent years) smokers, diabetics, HIV patients, cancer survivors, obese people, baby boomers, and teenage and elderly drivers.

Well, guess what? I think what constitutes a social burden is in the eye of the beholder. For example, I live in a city whose taxpayers recently voted to spend over half a billion dollars of their money to build two new professional sports stadiums. Was the cost of these stadiums to the general public a social burden? You bet it was, at least in my humble view, but others (in fact a slim majority of taxpayers) disagreed with me and voted for the new sports facilities. What about reckless politicians and greedy CEOs? Are they a "major burden to society?" I might think so; others might disagree. You see the problem with finger-pointing. Everything depends on your location and point of view.

So are the medical and social models incompatible? Not necessarily. The problem occurs when one person (or group of people) is perceived as, or reduced to, one particular medical condition. I mean, we all have medical conditions of one kind or another. For example, I have asthma, but does that mean I should be essentialized as an asthmatic? No, because I'm not JUST an asthmatic. I'm a jogger, a reader, a swimmer, and hundreds of other things. Clearly, I have an impairment: asthma. But there's a social component to my medical condition, because my impairment is made much worse by certain social environments (smoky, moldy, etc.). So it seems to me that, unless we essentialize or take a reductive either/or position, the medical and social models could, ideally, coexist.

Sam would probably disagree with me on this, as would most autistic activists and bloggers. Because he was born with hydrocephalus, Sam was medicalized from the moment of his birth. Early on, he enjoyed chatting with his pediatricians, not so much with his neurosurgeons. But by the time he entered puberty, Sam had his fill of doctors. He'd grown tired of their incessant questions, tired of always being the medical object. What he hated most was when they talked about him as if he weren't present. As though he were invisible.

After his second psych hospitalization, Sam became even more impatient with the medical establishment. Too many bad memories connected to doctors' offices and hospitals. On days when he knew he had an appointment, he would remain sullen and uncommunicative. Resentful. It became increasingly difficult to get him to any doctor, especially his psychiatrist. The only psychiatrist Sam had really tolerated was Dr. B. at the university hospital, who only saw in-patients. Finally, on our last aborted trip to see his shrink, Sam grabbed the steering wheel and started hitting me until I had no choice but to turn around and cancel the appointment. Since then, our family doctor has prescribed all of Sam's meds. It's difficult enough just to get him to our family doc without incident.

I see the same attitude toward doctors in the blogs I've mentioned here. Nearly all autistic bloggers have at least one medical horror story to share. Why the fear and resentment? I suspect it has something to do with the fact they're tired, and a little afraid, of the power of the medical establishment to control their lives. Once you start receiving ongoing treatment for a condition such as autism or epilepsy, you get caught up in a self-perpetuating medical apparatus that becomes almost impossible to escape from (much like cancer or HIV patients who feel swallowed up by the medical apparatus).

You're reduced to an autism patient, or an epilepsy patient. There's no freedom to define yourself as anything else but a patient. That is, no freedom to free yourself from the role of a passive patient who RECEIVES treatment. A medical object.

Then there's the problem of not being taken seriously. Listen to Elmindreda as she recounts one such trip to her doctor. Knowing she has difficulty communicating with doctors, she prepares a list of questions to ask and takes along a friend who "speaks NT" more fluently than she does and thus could "translate" when necessary. And sure enough, when Elmindreda begins to falter, halfway through her list, the doctor asks if she is "a fully healthy person." At that point her friend jumps in and informs the doctor that Elmindreda is autistic.

Suddenly, everything changed.

"Once autism was mentioned, he changed from speaking *to* me to speaking *of* me," she writes. "From claiming that there was nothing to be done, he now urged my friend that I needed to seek psychiatric help." Thus with the mere mention of the word autism, her medical issues had been transformed into psychiatric issues. Elmindreda confesses that a few moments later she had an anxiety attack caused by her anger and confusion.

This is a common experience for autistic and disabled people.

Doctors assume that autistic people can't speak for themselves, so they speak to parents or aides, whoever happens to be with the autistic person. The autistic person ceases to exist, becoming an object, a topic of conversation, not a subject.

In his NTs Are Weird blog, Joel Smith writes about the stress (as well as the fear factor) involved in seeing a doctor. He tells the story of a recent trip to his doctor and uses it as an example to generalize about the difficulties he and other autistic people have in seeking and obtaining medical care. The official reason for this particular doctor's visit was to ask for a refill of his allergy medication. But Smith happened to be sick at the time of the visit and wanted to tell the doctor about his symptoms, but he was prevented from doing so by an inability to initiate the conversation. In the end he never volunteered any information, because doing so would have been "far too stressful." As a consequence he came away without getting advice or medical care for whatever ailed him.

"I'd love to go to a doctor that understands autism and understands that ... we're not going to volunteer any information and thus you need to ask some probing questions," he writes. He adds that it would also be helpful if the doctor knew that he could be in great pain and not be able to talk about his pain.

Because of the inability to initiate communication and the inability to cope with stress, "medical care is not accessible to many of us," he writes. He adds that the solution is not incarceration or forced medication, but rather to ensure that autistic people are comfortable enough to cope with stress and to ask some direct questions about their health.

Reading Smith's post, I came away with a much better understanding of Sam's behavior at the doctor's office. Not only does Sam have the same difficulty communicating with doctors, for all the reasons mentioned above, he's virtually incapacitated by stress when he's in their presence. Often Sam will refuse (or be unable) to speak altogether. When a doctor asks him if he's feeling okay, for example, he'll turn to me:

"Am I?"

If I insist he respond, he might offer a brief answer. Then again, he might sit there staring at me until I have to break the awkward silence.

Something else about Smith's post opened my eyes. Like Smith, Sam can be in extreme pain and not say a word about his pain. Sam never complains about not feeling well, not even after he bangs his head. I used to think he had an extremely high tolerance for pain, but now I'm not so sure. Maybe the stress, the anxiety involved in talking about not feeling well (as well as the fear of being sent to a hospital) prevents him from acknowledging his medical needs and asking for help.

Of the other issues involved in medicalization, none is more controversial than drugs, especially psychiatric drugs. Autistic bloggers are probably more united on this issue than any other, with the lone exception of institutions. That is, united in opposition to forcing autistic people to take psychiatric drugs. Rants against what Cal Montgomery calls "the agitated stupor of drugs" run throughout the autistic blogosphere. From Ritalin and Prozac to new (and expensive) anti-psychotics like Risperdal, Seroquel, Zyprexa, and Geodon, bloggers tend to reject the drugs outright. They point out that autism is NOT a psychiatric illness.

Agreed.

And yet I can't totally accept the anti-drug argument. Yes, I think overmedication is a problem. And yes, I think more resources should be directed toward community services, supports, and other accommodations instead of to Big Pharma. We spend far too much money on drugs and not nearly enough on community services. I wouldn't argue with that.

Sometimes, though, the decision to medicate is not a matter of choice. Take Sam, for example. We tried to avoid giving him medications. But at the age of 13, with the onset of puberty, Sam had two grand mal seizures. We consulted a neurologist, who put Sam on Depakote (valproate), an anti-seizure medication that also helps regulate moods. Depakote has worked well for Sam. He hasn't had a seizure since he started taking the medication.

We resisted any additional drugs for about five years, until Sam's behavior spun out of control and he ended up on an adolescent psych ward at Children's Hospital. Psychiatrists there tried him on a number of the new anti-psychotics, searching for a magic drug that would allow him to control his violent outbursts. From the age of 18 through 22, Sam bounced from one psychiatrist to another, and from one new drug to another.

These were difficult years for Sam, because his psychiatrists couldn't just take him off one medication and prescribe another. One medication would have to be gradually withdrawn, while another was gradually added. Trial and error. After a while it became difficult to tell what worked and what didn't. After so many drugs, how could anyone tell?

This period of uncertainty lasted until Sam had his major breakdown at the age of 22. On the psych ward at the university hospital Sam finally found a combination that worked for him. His in-patient psychiatrist added Abilify (aripiprazole) and Lithium to the Depakote he was already taking. Abilify is a newer, atypical mood stabilizer; Lithium has been for decades the most effective medication to treat bipolar disorder.

Since then, Sam's drug regime hasn't changed. And the meds work. He's been stable for four years.

That's the upside.

There's also a downside. Like most people on these medications, Sam's weight has increased substantially. He's gone from a 30-inch to a 36-inch waist. To make matters worse, he's become acutely sensitive about how he looks, especially his weight. He'll ask if he's too heavy, if he's "obese."

"Do I need to lose weight?"

What do you say? I mean, the weight gain really isn't his fault. He can't control the side effects of his meds. But I do worry about diabetes and heart disease and the other health issues associated with being overweight. So I usually encourage him to TRY to control his weight, recognizing there's a limit to what he can do. You don't need to lose weight, I'll say. Just try not to gain any more.

The worst thing is when other people make careless remarks about Sam's weight. Not long ago a friend of ours, trying to be funny in a sarcastic way, greeted Sam by saying, "Sam, you're eating too many hot dogs!"

Our friend's insensitive remark still bothers Sam. "Why did he say that?" Sam asks. "Was he making fun of me?"

To drug or not to drug. Not an easy question to answer.

Still, all things considered, drugs have benefited Sam. Without them, he would not be living semi-independently. He knows that as well as anyone; he not only asks for his meds, he demands them.

While on vacation in South Beach a few years back, Sam found a T-shirt with a funny slogan that he repeats on occasion:

"WHERE THE F____ IS MY MEDICATION!"

Chapter 18

Institutionalization

He died seven years before Sam was born.

I knew him as cousin Ricky, four years my junior. Growing up, I spent many weekends playing with Ricky and his two older brothers. He played as hard as the rest of us; he was just a little slow and uncoordinated. Sometimes he would slur his speech when he talked. Even as a kid I knew Ricky was "different," but so were lots of other people in my small Midwestern town, people with various disabilities and injuries, including several veterans injured in World War II.

I was told that Ricky had a degenerative muscle disorder. His parents called it Muscular Dystrophy, but I have no idea if that was the official diagnosis. Diagnoses tended to be rather vague back then in the staid, button-down 1950s. Also, my aunt and uncle, like most people then, tended to cover up family affairs that were thought to be embarrassing or shameful. When it came to anything that would reflect badly on the family, people tended to be secretive, if not downright evasive.

By the time we entered adolescence, my cousins and I had gone our separate ways, pursuing the many pleasures of the 1960s. I rarely saw my aunt and uncle except at large family gatherings where no one ever mentioned Ricky. He seemed to have disappeared, fallen off the face of the earth. Then one day I asked about Ricky's absence and was told, matter-of-factly, that he had been sent away to a state institution. Just like that. Gone. But why?

I was shocked and dismayed. I had no idea they were even considering such a move. To me, it was inconceivable that they could they do this to their son, my cousin. I remember feeling vaguely guilty whenever I thought about Ricky, especially when everyone else in the family seemed to pretend that Ricky had never existed. Maybe it was just too painful for my aunt and uncle to talk about the son they'd sent away, other than to say it was "for his own good."

Whenever I would hear that rationalization, I would ask myself, "How can sending someone to a state institution be for the person's own good?"

A few years later Ricky died, disappearing forever from the family consciousness. I remember being told that he drowned in a shallow stream that ran through the wooded grounds of the state institution that he knew as home. No one could explain how he came to be at the stream or how he drowned. No one talked about him after his death, just as no one had talked about him when he was alive. Richard Wilson died in December 1973. He was 21 years old.

Today I'm still troubled by the thought of Ricky and the life he might have led. If he'd been born only a decade or so later, he most certainly wouldn't have died face down in that shallow stream. By then, medical science had developed a better understanding of how to treat degenerative muscle disorders, and disabled children weren't as routinely or as casually institutionalized.

But back in the 1950s, parents were encouraged to either keep their disabled children hidden away at home or, better yet, institutionalize them. Medical professionals and state workers counseled parents that disabled kids were better off with their own "kind." Likewise, institutionalization was better for the rest of the family, which would be spared undue stress and the possibility of being "contaminated" by the defective family member. A state facility would provide the necessary moral quarantine.

"Medical experts writing in popular magazines and books insisted that parents not feel guilty about their retarded children;

instead, they advised parents who could not cope to put their retarded children away and forget about them," writes James W. Trent, Jr. in his comprehensive history, *Inventing the Feeble Mind: A History of Mental Retardation in the United States.* "In a time when professional (and especially medical) advice was never so revered, parents took the counsel seriously."

Several important popular books of the early 1950s reinforced this trend, telling parents it was "okay" to institutionalize their disabled children. Pearl S. Buck's *The Child Who Never Grew* (1950) started what one historian has called the "Parent-Confessional Genre of the 1950s." In her book Buck revealed a secret that she had kept hidden from the public for over 20 years: that her daughter, born with phenylketonuria (PKU) had lived at the Vineland Training School (a private institution) since 1928. Since Buck had won the Nobel Prize for literature, her advice to other "bewildered and ashamed parents" carried enormous weight. So, too, did John P. Frank's advice in *My Son's Story* (1952). A professor of American constitutional law, Frank tells the story of how he and his wife came to the decision to place their "retarded" son Petey (at the age of 19 months) in Saint Rita's Home in Wisconsin. Other accounts followed, including Dale Evans Rogers' *Angel Unaware* (1953), a book about Dale Evans and Roy Roger's daughter Robin, who was born with Down Syndrome and who died from mumps and encephalitis at the age of two.

As a result of both professional and peer pressure, vulnerable people like my cousin Ricky were locked away in dreary state institutions, most of which dated from the 1930s or before. Some were remnants of the farm colonies so popular during the 1910s and 1920s. Most disabled people who entered these institutions never left. They died, like Ricky, in the institution. Many were buried on the grounds of the institution.

From today's perspective, it's hard to imagine anyone sent to one of these institutions would be better off with his/her own "kind." In an earlier chapter, we heard Amanda Baggs and Cal Montgomery talk about their traumatic experiences in institutions, as well as their fear of being sent back to a state facility. In essence the de-institutionalization movement of the 1970s and 1980s (in favor of community placement) was an acknowledgement that state institutions had failed to adequately care for their patients.

The same skepticism applies to the 1950s notion that families would be better off if they institutionalized their disabled children, as if institutionalization was in itself a magic solution that would cure an over-burdened, stressed-out family. Again, from today's perspective, it's hard to imagine that such banishment would be so easy and breezy, so quick and painless for the other family members involved. What happens, emotionally and psychologically, to a family that permanently institutionalizes a son or daughter?

Journalist John Hockenberry, an Emmy and two-time Peabody Award winner while reporting for National Public Radio, ABC News, and NBC News, has written a sobering account of how such a decision affected his family. In his memoir, *Moving Violations*, Hockenberry writes about visiting an uncle who had been institutionalized since 1943. Born with PKU and said to be hopelessly "retarded," uncle Charlie was sent away as a small child, supposedly for the good of the family. From that moment on the family had to live with the pain, anguish, and guilt caused by their decision. Hardly the good that was imagined.

The fact that Hockenberry is himself disabled, having been paraplegic since an auto accident at the age of 19, gives his account an added intensity. He reflects on the confluence of his and his uncle's lives: "Our lives are lived in the crawl space between our strangeness and other people's reactions and fears. The instinctive human fear of those who are different has defined both of our lives. The forces that put my uncle away would also place me in a category from which there is no escape. Inside me is the engine that thrashes about never stopping, always mindful that someday those same forces could decide my fate, claim that I am really helpless, that my life is not worth living, give me a label, and send me away to a place for all those like me."

The visit turns out to be anticlimactic. He doesn't recognize his

160

uncle. His uncle doesn't recognize him. Still, while sitting with his uncle, Hockenberry has a revelation: "In the end, there was no metaphor for Charlie. The most important thing was simply to be there near him and allow who he really was to sink in. If I really wanted to know him, I had to sit quietly and listen to the details of his life, something people so rarely do. Just as people looked for the shortcuts for knowing about my life in a wheelchair, I was looking for the same thing to understand my uncle Charlie. I was staring now. I was human, just like him."

Indeed.

I'm in no position to judge anyone else. People do what they have to do, I suppose. But here's my view. If inclusion as a concept means anything, it has to apply to more than just educational opportunities. I'm not saying inclusion at school isn't important; obviously it is. But so is inclusion in one's family, and in social and public life.

At the risk of sounding moralistic, it seems to me that all children have a right to be included in the lives of their families. After all, children don't choose to be born. On the contrary, parents choose to have children, and along with that choice comes the responsibility to love and care for the children they bring into the world. Sending a disabled child away because the child has a disability is a violation of parental responsibility. I'm not talking about disabled adults, who need and in most cases want independence. That's a different, more complicated situation.

Consider what happens to the institutionalized child. The child is effectively cut off from family identity and family history, thereby making it difficult if not impossible for the child to develop a personal identity and a personal history. But institutionalization does more damage than that; it denies the child a social life, a connection to the larger world. This is a terrible loss since we are all social animals, as the saying goes. Without a social and public life, the child loses the opportunity to grow personally and socially. For all real purposes, development ends in the institution. The child becomes the institution.

In his groundbreaking 1961 book, *Asylum: Essays on the Social Situation of Mental Patients and Other Inmates*, sociologist Erving Goffman described the process of dehumanization that occurs in institutions. Because they are "total institutions," these asylums strip away their patients' individuality and provoke deviant reactions from them. Labeled deviants, institutionalized patients react accordingly, becoming more suspicious, depressed, hostile, anxious, and bewildered, thus confirming the label. In the end, the institution produces the very behaviors that it purports to control.

Sometimes I think of my cousin Ricky and wonder what kind of life he might have had if he hadn't been institutionalized. If he were alive today, he would be 55 years old. Would he look the same, just older and grayer? Would he live in a real community, among people who accepted and cared for him? Would he have friends? Companions? A partner?

It's obvious, I suppose, that in thinking about Ricky I'm also thinking about Sam. I find myself wishing I had a crystal ball, so that I could peer at Sam 20 years into the future. Will he have found his own community? Will he have the supports and services that community placement requires? By this I mean state and federal government supports, not charitable and religious. Sam is not an object of charity. I repeat, disabled people are NOT objects of charity.

Government supports and services are the key to everything. Without the necessary supports and services, community placement is a cruel and empty promise. People end up as isolated as they were in the institutions, perhaps even more isolated. They find themselves adrift without jobs or money or medical care, without aides or companions or friends. Many end up on the streets, without what most of us would call a life.

You can empty the institutions, but that's not the same thing as providing a real community that will meet the needs of real people.

Chapter 19

Surf's Up

So here we come rolling through the parking garage, across the access road, and into the terminal. Sam brings up the rear, wearing his backpack and pulling his suitcase on wheels along behind him. He walks slowly, deliberately, with a certain look fixed on his face. Whether it's determination, concentration, or horror, I can't tell. He stares straight ahead, refusing to look from side to side. When he comes to a curb or a cutout, he stops to take a look, and then yanks the suitcase over the hump.

By the time we get to the ticketing and baggage counter, Sam lags far behind. But no matter, he's still moving forward, staring straight ahead. He doesn't stop until his suitcase bumps into my suitcase and clunks down on the floor. It's taken a great effort on his part to get here, but now he's ready to roll. Miami here we come! Except for one thing.

"Are we through security yet?" he asks.

"No, that's next," I say.

He gets a worried look on his face. He hates security.

"Don't worry. We're early, the lines are still short."

He doesn't really believe me (for good reason), but he waits patiently until we get our boarding passes and baggage tickets. He's a real trooper, at least until we get to security.

If Sam panics, it's always at security. The lines are bad enough, but having to take his shoes off and go through the Puffer machine can send him off the deep end. By the time we clear security, all of us are exhausted. Especially Sam. He's tense, irritable, on the edge of a meltdown.

That is, he's edgy until he sees the McDonald's and Pizza Hut signs, which perk him up immediately. On the return trip he looks for the Uno's sign at the Miami International Airport. He has them all memorized. We always stop to get Sam a snack and soft drink. It's a routine we established when Sam was young, as a reward for his hard work. Why stop now? Sam loves his snacks.

Once he gets to the gate, Sam's fine. Sitting down, he opens his backpack and spreads out his stuff: portable CD player, CDs, *USA Today* weather page. Now he can kick back and enjoy his rituals. Minutes later he's humming to himself, happy to be on his way to Miami.

Like many autistic people, Sam has had his difficulties with travel. As much as possible, we've tried to organize our trips so that he'll feel comfortable on vacations. Sam needs to get away, because he works hard at keeping himself together every single day. Early on he had difficulty with vacations to big cities. We tried New York, Washington, Chicago, Atlanta, San Francisco, Los Angeles, and San Diego, all of which overloaded Sam with loud noises and aggressive crowds. Not good.

So we tried beach resorts, several of them, before falling in love with South Beach. Or rather, Sam decided on South Beach. Why? Because J-Lo, Snoop Dogg, and a host of other rappers party in South Beach, so why not the Family Gangsta? Sure, the warm weather, the great restaurants, and the rich street life provide an added incentive, but it's the gangsta flavor that Sam likes most about what he calls "the party capitol of the world!"

Every year now we spend Christmas week in South Beach, where Sam has had only positive experiences. This is a big deal, because once he has a bad time somewhere, he refuses to go back. We would never get him on the plane.

To make traveling easier for Sam, we follow the same exact routine every year. After a short, direct flight to the Miami International Airport, we take a taxi to Sam's hotel of choice. He loves the

Palms, a small Four Star hotel with a mostly European clientele and a fabulous ocean-front. Its enclosed grounds come complete with pool, cabana bar and restaurant, lots of palm trees, and two parrots who talk to him. We've been there so often that even the parrots recognize Sam.

When we get to our room, Sam follows a well-established, ritualized process. You could almost call it a form of colonization. What I mean is that he uses his rituals to re-familiarize the room, to make it the same as it was last year and the year before. To subdue the space and make it familiar. To make it his space.

First, he digs through the drawers of the bureau and nightstand to find the Miami telephone directory. Then he browses through the residence, business, and yellow page sections looking for certain people and businesses. Especially pizza restaurants. When he's finished with his initial evaluation, he tosses the books on the floor, where they will remain until later that night when he'll do a more thorough read-through.

Next, he plops down in the room's biggest, most comfortable chair, unzips his backpack, and retrieves his portable CD player. Stacks of CDs follow. Within minutes, he'll have CDs spread out on the floor and on the nearest table. Then he'll listen to a song or two from NWA or another of his favorite groups. Not an entire CD, just a couple of tunes to break in the room and establish his territory. He'll get back to his music later, after he finishes with the telephone directory.

Then it's time for a soft drink and, depending on the time of day, off to the beach or the restaurants. By that time Sam has debriefed and acclimatized himself to the South Beach lifestyle. Once he's re-established his routines, he's comfortable. He can relax and have a good time.

To help him cope, we follow the same schedule each day. After breakfast, Cindy and I walk on the boardwalk while Sam reads the *Miami Herald*, looking for notices of the latest rapper sightings. Just last year the venerable Snoop Dogg partied in South Beach while we were there, providing Sam with some good reading material.

About 10 A.M. we head to the beach with a picnic lunch. Sam spreads out his stuff on one of the chaises provided by the hotel. He has his CD player and CDs and whatever else he's brought along. He mostly listens to his rap music while we read, although occasionally he'll want to wade into the ocean. Well, tiptoe would be more like it. Once he gets in over his ankles, he grabs on to whomever he's with and bolts for shore, one whole step backward. Even small waves bother Sam. He doesn't like the feeling of the sand eroding under his feet. Sometimes, to avoid losing his footing, he'll sit down on the sand and let the waves wash over his legs. "Surf's up!" he'll say, as though he were riding a surfboard.

Some days on the beach he'll entertain himself by people watching. And people listening. You hear lots of languages on South Beach, especially French, Italian, German, Spanish, and Portuguese. Sam likes to listen in to some of the conversations, even though he can't understand them. When it comes to the topless Brazilian babes, he feigns disinterest. But if you watch long enough, you'll catch him checking them out from time to time.

By 1 P.M. Sam has gone though his repertoire of rap CDs. He's bored and ready to move on to the next pleasure: the pool. So we pack up and head back to the hotel pool, surrounded by tall, cool palms and tropical plantings. Most of the hotel employees know Sam by now, so they'll chat with him about the weather. He'll tell everyone he meets, for the umpteenth time, that we're from Cincinnati, where the weather sucks. That's why we're here, he wants everyone to know. He'll also say hello to the bilingual parrots, who speak both English and Spanish. "*Hola*! Polly want a cracker?"

"*Hola ... Hola ... Hola*," the parrots screech.

After he says hello to everyone, Sam's ready for a swim. So he eases himself into the pool and jumps around with whomever he's with, Cindy or I, until he gets bored with that and wants to come out. Snoop Dogg, Ludacris, or Jay-Z tend to be better company than his parents any old day.

Usually about 3 P.M. we've all had too much sun, so Sam leads the way back to our room, by way of the gift shop/snack bar. After showers, we do some afternoon shopping and then, around 5 P.M., start down the boardwalk to the restaurants. The walk to Lincoln Avenue takes about 45 minutes, but if we decide to walk all the way to the tip of South Beach on Ocean Drive, it takes us over an hour. Good exercise, especially for Sam, who tends to mellow out when he walks. And the boardwalk, unlike the street, provides a quiet, stress-free environment for Sam.

We eat dinner early, Sam's insistence. Then it's on to the gelato shops and the street scene. Sam likes street music, even if it's not gangsta rap. But whatever he's doing, he always checks his watch every so often just to make sure he leaves in time to make it back to the hotel by his usual bedtime. Even on vacation Sam sticks to his schedule. If he's not in bed by 10 P.M., he'll turn into a pumpkin. An angry pumpkin.

Next day, same thing. We might vary our routine on Christmas morning, but otherwise one day resembles another. The only exception would be a rain-out, a rare event in South Beach, in which case we spend the afternoon at the cinema.

Most people would find our vacation much too regimented, but when you travel with Sam, regimented is good. Not only good, it's a necessity.

Given his routine, Sam relaxes in South Beach like nowhere else. In almost every photo taken of him since he hit puberty, Sam presents a tense, tortured face to the camera. But not at South Beach. Photos taken of him there show an incredibly relaxed, comfortable demeanor. It's like night and day. If only we could capture the sun, the fresh air, the exercise, and everything else and take it all back with us, I could almost imagine Sam being as consistently happy and content at home as he is in South Beach.

There's something else about South Beach that makes it so good for Sam. It's the diversity, the cosmopolitanism. With diversity comes a freedom from conventional attitudes and values, a freedom that Sam finds liberating. For a week he's free of the stigma of being autistic and disabled. He's just another odd, atypical character running around the beaches and restaurants. Another party animal.

No doubt about it, Sam's at his best in South Beach. When he's relaxed, he's extroverted and social. He makes friends with hotel staff and some of the guests who don't mind a few weather questions. Over the years he's befriended some interesting folks. For example, one year at the hotel's Christmas morning buffet we met a foxy Santa Claus, who Sam promptly dubbed the Bad Santa (after the movie of the same name). This Santa had a bad joke for everyone and a kiss (or two) for each of the ladies. But when Sam locked horns with him, the mischievous Santa fessed up about lots of stuff, including the fact that originally he was from the Cincinnati area. What was he doing incognito in Miami? The same thing we were, he said.

"Is it the weather?" Sam asked.

"That too!" he said.

The Bad Santa scored high on Sam's list of all-time interesting characters.

But the most remarkable person Sam ever met at South Beach was a young man named Stephen. Sam and Stephen took an immediate liking to each other. An English lad, about 30 years old, Stephen was on vacation with his parents. We noticed the parents first, because they spent every day poolside, their pale skin getting redder by the hour. Not Stephen. He would show up at the pool from time to time, wearing dress shorts and a polo shirt tucked neatly into his pants. A dapper dude, as Sam would say. The slightest affect of a developmental delay made him all the more interesting to Sam. A fellow traveler.

Stephen would chat with his parents for only a minute or two before heading back up to his room. Apparently he was too busy doing something to waste his days at the pool. He always noticed Sam, however. And one day he came over to introduce himself.

"I'm in men's wear," he said in a proper English accent when Sam asked what he did. It turned out that Stephen worked with his father, who owned a men's wear factory.

"I'm in weather," Sam responded. "But I like rap music too."

Later that day Stephen came back down to the pool carrying a sheet of paper. He sat down at our table and asked, "Does Sam like sirens?"

Sam's eyes lit up as though they were irradiated from within. Oh yeah!

Then Stephen handed Sam a technical spec sheet for a siren. "I made you a copy," Stephen said, and then proceeded to tell Sam all about the siren, which was available online, if Sam wanted to buy one.

"Tornado sirens?"

"Yeah, and fire sirens."

Sam sat across from Stephen, spellbound. He couldn't believe he'd actually met another person all eaten up by sirens. Nirvana.

Stephen seemed to know everything about sirens, all the specs of all the models for sale online. No wonder he was too busy to swim. He had way too much research to do.

For the next several days Sam and Stephen engaged in a running conversation about sirens that touched on just about anything anyone would ever want to know about sirens. Finally one day Stephen's mother joined us at our table. She explained that yes, Stephen had a 'thing' for sirens, and yes, he had a room full of actual sirens he'd ordered online, and yes, he set them off from time to time, following a set of rules they'd devised. Time of day, duration, that sort of thing.

She threw up her hands and asked, "What are you going to do?"

Cindy and I threw up our hands. "What are you going to do?"

Stephen left with his parents a day or so later, but not before he gave Sam spec sheets for a few more sirens, complete with instructions on how to order them online.

"You need a siren, Sam," Stephen said in parting. "You need to be prepared."

Every year since their fateful meeting Sam has looked for Stephen in South Beach. We see the Bad Santa most years, but not Stephen. We guess he's back in England with his sirens, doing more research so he can buy more sirens. Online.

When our week in South Beach comes to an end, all of us are ready to go home. Sam especially. He's anxious to get back to his buds and his regular social outings. Plus, he's looking forward to spending time in the Yellow Submarine, away from his parents.

So looking tan and fit, his energy renewed, Sam stuffs his CD player and CDs, now coated with sand, into his backpack. He doesn't much care about his clothes, but his CDs are another story. He checks under and behind all the furniture, knowing full well that he's lost more than a few discs over the years. He's left behind some Snoop Dogg from Santa Barbara to South Beach and lots of places in between.

With one last glance at the ocean, spread out in panorama outside the window of our ocean front room, he grabs his suitcase and follows us to the elevator and down to the lobby. Sam says goodbye to the doorman and everyone else we see in the lobby. Then we hail a taxi and zip off to the airport, where we arrive 20 minutes later. We're all a bit sad to find ourselves in line again, our Christmas vacation over for another year.

But wait. There's one more item on Sam's agenda, one more name on his dance card. Uno's!

Once we're through the hassle of security, Sam makes a bee-line to the Uno's Express. Doesn't matter what time of day it happens to be, Sam needs a pepperoni pie and a soft drink to ease of pain of leaving South Beach.

We arrive at the gate with plenty of time to spare. Sam doesn't like to be rushed, especially with an Uno's pizza in hand.

While we wait for the boarding call, we check off our list of pleasures enjoyed at South Beach. Only one tasty morsel missing. Stephen!

But who knows? Maybe next year.

Speaking of Stephen, Sam wants to know, "Do I really need a siren? To be prepared?"

Cindy rolls her eyes.

"Yeah, I know," Sam says. "When monkeys fly out my butt."

Chapter 20

Representation Politics

"Nothing about us, without us."

That's one of the central demands of the disability rights movement. Disabled people want to speak for and represent themselves. As they should.

But with autism, this demand is often overlooked. Why? Because neuro-typicals assume that most autistic people are nonverbal and mentally retarded. This ableist attitude denies autistic people the opportunity to speak for themselves. Instead, doctors, parents, and other "caregivers" presume to speak for autistic people and for autism in general.

I confronted this issue recently when someone from my university asked me to serve on a panel discussion of *The Curious Incident of the Dog in the Night-Time* by Mark Haddon. As part of diversity week, this particular panel would focus on autism, with Haddon's book serving as a point of entry. *Curious Incident* features a 15-year-old hero named Christopher who happens to be autistic. My panel would include autism experts from the medical school and other professionals knowledgeable about the disorder. I was asked because of my experience with Sam and because of my work in the academic field of Disability Studies.

I hesitated. After all, *Curious Incident* is a work of fiction written by a neuro-typical. Why not read something written by an autistic person? Lots of names came to mind: Temple Grandin, Donna Williams, Amanda Baggs, Cal Montgomery, and lots of others.

And something else bothered me. Why hadn't any autistic people been asked to join the panel? I mean, autistic people aren't that hard to find. As a matter of fact, my department had two graduate students with Asperger's, one of whom had been in two of my classes. I expressed my concerns to the panel organizer and volunteered to ask one of these students to participate in the discussion. I felt we needed to include someone who could talk about the actual lived experience of autism.

Well, as I soon discovered, the organizers were more interested in an "informed" medical opinion than whatever an autistic person had to say about living with autism. Let's just say that my suggestions were not well received. The audience would want information on autism research, as well as definitions, suspected causes, risk factors, diagnostic tests, treatments and all the other routine information that (I pointed out) was readily available on dozens of websites. As for including actual autistic people, the fictional Christopher was as real as they wanted!

The non-inclusion of autistic people on any panel or forum dedicated to autism strikes me as outrageously patronizing and insensitive, an example of ableism at its worst. I would also add that non-inclusion seems counter-productive. I mean, if you're going to have a panel discussion focused on one group of people, how can you have the discussion without a representative from that group? You would be missing the key ingredient: the lived experience of being autistic, gay, female, single parent, or whatever. Neuro-typicals would understand a lot more about autism if they would only listen to autistic people.

Zilari addresses this subject in her Processing in Parts blog. She suggests, ever so politely, that autistic people just might be able to offer some insights into autistic behaviors. She prefaces her comment by saying that she would never claim to speak for everyone on the spectrum. "However, I do think that autistic people can, in some cases, better assess how another autistic person is thinking or feeling at a given moment based on common experience and similar body language / information coding," she writes.

Her post recounts an incident involving a woman and her autistic daughter. The woman had driven her daughter to school following their routine, but the daughter refused to get out of the car. The perplexed mother couldn't understand why the daughter had refused. Zilari's response on hearing the story was that something must have been different that day; perhaps the usual cue that prompted the girl to get out of the car was absent. Sure enough, on reflection, the girl's mother realized she'd forgotten to hand her daughter her backpack — the last thing that usually happened before the girl got out of the car and went into the school.

If I had read Zilari's post a few years earlier, I might have avoided a similar situation. Here's what happened.

During Sam's high school years, I drove him to school every morning. Most days he rode the school bus home in the afternoon (unless I had to come get him early). I dropped him off at the same spot — a sidewalk that led directly to a door next to his learning center. Once inside the door, he only had to turn left and walk a few steps down the hall to find his classroom. He'd done it so many times that he could do it in his sleep.

On this particular day, during Sam's tenth grade year, I went to drop him off at the usual spot but found a bus unloading students parked there, blocking access to the sidewalk. I parked behind the bus, thinking that Sam could get to the sidewalk by walking around the bus. That meant he would have to walk across some grass, a distance of no more than 20 feet. No big deal, right?

Wrong. Sam would not get out of the car. When I told him I'd walk with him across the grass, he screamed, "NO!" and banged his head against the side window.

So now, stressed out, I looked around quickly for a backup plan. I spotted another sidewalk that led from a parking lot at the end of the building to that same door. Bingo, I thought. But again, when I drove into the parking lot and parked alongside the building, not two steps from this other sidewalk, Sam refused to budge. No way.

I should have known better. I don't know why I was so dense.

But I tried to reason with Sam, saying I would walk with him to the door. "Look, we're even closer here. You don't have to walk so far." My bad.

"NOOOOO!" Sam screamed, banging his head repeatedly against the side window.

"Okay, we'll go back," I said, trying to talk him down.

We ended up driving around the building a few times until the bus blocking our sidewalk had finished unloading its students. When I stopped the car Sam didn't say a word. He hopped out of his seat and walked off by himself, ambling slowly toward the door. Just before he stepped inside, he turned and waved goodbye. Just like that. As if it were any other ordinary day.

Autistic writers and bloggers have produced a considerable body of work that attempts to explain autism to non-autistics. Some of the better-known writers are Temple Grandin and Donna Williams, whose works I've mentioned in previous chapters. Highly praised recent memoirs include David Tammet's *Born on a Blue Day*; Ralph Savarese's *Reasonable People: A Memoir of Autism and Adoption*; and Jerry Newport, Mary Newport, and Johnny Dodd's *Mozart and the Whale*.

On the whole autistic bloggers tend to be more radical than Grandin, Williams, Tammet, and the others. Bloggers vent their anger at parents, doctors, and other neuro-typicals who would presume to speak for autistic people. But the bloggers save their harshest words for non-autistic run advocacy organizations like Autism Speaks and Autism Society of America. These organizations claim to speak for autism, though their representations of autism are hardly flattering to autistic people.

The Autistic Bitch from Hell has remained one of the staunchest critics of Autism Speaks and its co-founders, Suzanne and Bob Wright. In one post from her blog, "Autism Speaks and Stigma," she writes about having seen a recent interview with Suzanne Wright in which she claimed that her organization seeks to raise awareness of autism in order to "take the stigma off." That comment didn't set well with the Autistic Bitch from Hell, who argues that Autism Speaks has created more stigma against autistic people than any other entity. "The consistent message put forth by Autism Speaks has been that autistic people are tragically defective burdens on society and that a child would be better off dead than autistic," she writes.

Similarly, Cal Montgomery criticizes both Autism Speaks and the Autism Society of America. In an essay for *Ragged Edge* magazine entitled "Autistics Speak," Montgomery points out that "ASA calls itself the 'voice of autism' in order to attract more money." She continues: "I'm the last person to start a 'No representation without communication' movement. But I've known enough people who have opposed what nondisabled people have to say on their behalf, and enough people who have opposed what more privileged disabled people have to say on their behalf, to be wary of anyone — anyone — who claims the right to speak on behalf of others chosen in part because of their presumed inability to consent. Especially when the constituency has to be repeatedly gerrymandered to exclude dissenters. Especially when the constituency's reported interests strongly resemble what's good for the spokesperson."

She concludes by repeating her initial point: "And these campaigns are designed to get you to send money."

I don't want to mislead by implying that all bloggers agree on who has the right to speak for autism. They don't. In fact, they disagree on lots of issues. The autistic blogosphere seems to break into two main camps: aspies and auties (to use their terminology). Aspies, or people with Asperger's, sometimes insist on separating themselves from auties, or autistic people. The aspie stereotype goes something like this: "high-functioning" savants, good with numbers but not so good with people, proud of who they are and opposed to a hypothetical cure for autism. In contrast, here's the autie stereotype: "low-functioning" autistics, not good with numbers or people, with little or no ability to communicate and open to the possibility of a cure. Don't get me wrong; these are only stereotypes, no more accurate than any other stereotypes.

Generally speaking, aspies don't like to be called auties.

Likewise, auties don't like to be called aspies. Amanda Baggs, an autie, has written several posts about being misidentified as an aspie. Many people assume she has Asperger's because of her prolific writing and her obvious intelligence. She calls this stereotyping "aspification." On the other hand, aspies take pride in being aspies and resent being identified as supposedly lower-functioning auties. Call it the War of the Aspies.

Some autistic activists find the divide in the autism community problematic, even self-defeating. For example, the Autistic Bitch from Hell has written a post that warns both sides not to lose sight of the overall goal of autism activism. She writes in her blog: "The autistic civil rights movement is becoming increasingly divided into two factions." One faction, which she refers to as the "pride faction," sees autistic people as a social minority and stresses the importance of positive language and inspirational role models. The other faction, which she calls the anti-elitists, maintains that there are genuine difficulties associated with autism and that focusing too much on pride and accomplishments could result in discrimination against or lack of services for less fortunate autistic people.

The Autistic Bitch from Hell calls both viewpoints "reasonable" so long as they are not treated as contradictory or mutually exclusive. She cautions that it should be possible to avoid the use of "unnecessarily negative language" while still acknowledging the existence of actual difficulties.

So much for the idea of a monolithic autism community.

Like most people on the autism spectrum, Sam has both aspie and autie characteristics. Remember, ASDs are not either/or; they're a spectrum. To most people Sam initially appears to be an aspie because he's smart and a good talker. But as people get to know Sam, recognizing his visual and fine-motor difficulties as well as his behavior issues, they assume the opposite: that he's an autie.

Sam doesn't use either of these terms. Obviously, he knows he's disabled. He'll rigorously defend disabled people if he hears a cutting or ableist remark. And yet he doesn't like it when other people identify him as disabled. That is, he doesn't like to be categorized and classified. He knows very well what assumptions underlie such categories and classifications. He understands the stigma.

So Sam speaks only for himself, not for anyone else. Certainly not for the group, whatever group that would be.

Neither does Sam like it when someone speaks for him. Living with Sam, I've been trained to butt OUT of his conversations. Except with doctors, who conjure up too many bad memories, Sam isn't shy about speaking up for himself. He'll say anything to anyone, if he's in the right mood. In fact, sometimes he won't even allow me to speak to his other companions when they get back from dinner or a movie. That's his territory. His life.

· Sam makes it clear that I'm not invited.

"Why would Mike want to talk to you?" Sam will ask, for example. "You're not his friend."

"Hey, I'm just trying to be social," I might say, trying to defend myself.

Likewise, when Sam's companions arrive, he has to be the one who greets them at the door. He wants to tell them the news of the day, everything from the weather report to what his parents have planned to what time the mail came. Sam likes to be in charge of delivering all the news. He's his own news anchor, meteorologist, and gossip columnist combined.

Back before Sam was the Family Gangsta, during his junior and high school years, he did a lot of free writing. Self expression. He wrote stories and poems about himself, his family, and his friends. One poem, in particular, struck me as something special because it revealed so much about Sam. Entitled "Detention," Sam wrote the poem during the years when he was forever getting in trouble by violating the personal space of his aides and teachers. The result was a plaintive poem about always getting busted:

Detention:
Oh, no. Not again.
I feel bad 'cause I lost my cool.
I should have taken a time out,

I should have done what I was supposed to do.
"Come on in, Sam," the principal says.
He doesn't mean his office.
There's another room he takes me to,
a small room just for me.

What did you do?
he wants to know.
So I tell him.
I like talking to the principal
better than taking my time outs.
Maybe I can stay here,
instead of going back to class
instead of doing what I was supposed to do.
I just hope he doesn't give me
an after school detention.
                                    — Sam Wilson

The poem is endearing for so many reasons. The fact that Sam remembers being taken to another room, "a small room just for me," not the principal's office. The fact that he likes talking to the principal and hopes he can stay there shooting the breeze instead of going back to class and doing what he was supposed to do. The poem says a lot about his priorities: his wonderful ability to form social relationships, even in the most awkward and unlikely circumstances, and his lack of interest in what was happening back in the classroom. So, too, does his fear of an after school detention say a lot about Sam. He's too full of life to be held after school. To Sam, an after school detention would be cruel (but not unusual) punishment.

In another poem, aptly entitled "Personal Space," we can see how hard Sam works at controlling his tactile issues:

Personal Space:
So hard to control
getting into my aide's

personal space.
No touching, no grabbing
don't want to lose my face.

Just relax,
take a time out.
Don't worry, don't be nervous.
Got to tell myself,
"Sam, don't do it!"

Oh, such a pretty lady ...
I wish I could think of something else,
like baseball, like pizza, like a hot fudge sundae.
Why can't I learn about
personal space?
— Sam Wilson

Over the years I've been amazed at all I've learned from listening to Sam. In particular, I remember Sam's performance at his Independent Transition Program meeting after high school. Designed to help Sam plan his future, the ITP meeting included people from the county MRDD, the local workshop that Sam was scheduled to begin attending, and other members of Sam's "team."

Using a poster size sheet of paper and a set of colored markers, the team leader drew a "map" of how Sam would get from high school to the future Sam imagined for himself. He wrote, "Sam Wilson — Thinking About the Future," at the top of the map. Everyone at the meeting that day contributed valuable ideas, which the team leader dutifully added to the road map. But Sam was clearly in charge. He was bubbling with excitement and letting his imagination run wild. It was as though the poster represented a magic wishing board where everything Sam put down would come true, presto, just like that.

The result: a cartographic representation of Sam's hopes and dreams.

By the time Sam's map was finished, it included some real gems. For example, Sam would live in a "cool apartment," but not with just any old roommates. No, he wanted either a "girlfriend" or a "sexy roommate." Moreover, in this cool apartment, Sam expected to have the usual stuff including "lots of bathrooms" and a really "big stereo."

How would he support himself? By taking a few classes at a community college and then "working as little as possible." When? In a year or two.

To hear Sam tell it, he had a game plan for the rest of his life. The only speed bump on the road to success was an upcoming stint at the workshop.

Sam's performance that day gave me an insight into his imagination.

What was so fascinating was how Sam imagined his future. Basically, he wanted the same things as any other 20-year-old male. Why wouldn't he? As Sam says, "Guys just want to have fun."

Of course, our road map of Sam's future didn't look terribly realistic a few weeks later when he was kicked out of the workshop.

I took the ejection harder than he did. Sam didn't seem to care. His enthusiasm for the future was undiminished.

"It's okay, the workshop wasn't for me, Dad," he said one day, trying to console me. I appreciated the gesture, even though I felt I was the one who should be offering consolation. The irony wasn't lost on Sam, who gave me a big smile.

In retrospect, I know he was right about the workshop. It wasn't for him. So where does that leave his road map?

The other day I rummaged through my file cabinet and pulled out "Sam Wilson — Thinking about the Future," a bit tattered and yellowed with age but still intact, more or less. When I unrolled the map and spread it out on my desk, I saw something I hadn't noticed before. The stick figure representing Sam wasn't stationary but was a blur of motion, moving lickety-split, picking up speed with every stride. The boldly drawn speed lines and arrows propelled stick figure Sam quickly through the workshop and out the other side, where the caption reads: "On my way to..."

And that, of course, is the big question. To where? But the more I thought about it, the more I began to realize that the important thing wasn't the destination — it was much too early to think about a destination. The important thing was that Sam was in motion, moving forward, on his way to whatever destination he would ultimately choose.

Chapter 21

Resentment

Though Sam and I have reached an accommodation, more or less, we still have issues that arise from time to time. The nastiest: resentment. Sam resents having to depend on others for assistance, especially me now that he has officially designated me a "geezer." He'll often tell me to get lost. "Can't you go somewhere?" he'll ask. "Go check e-mail, or go run some errands. I'm tired of looking at you!" Sometimes just the sight of me seems to put him in a bad mood. But when I go, he resents me for not being there when he needs something. "Where were you?" he'll ask, standing in the garage waiting when I drive up. "My television stopped working" (translation: he can't find the remote). Or even more catastrophic: "My Walkman needs new batteries." It's a Catch-22 situation. He only wants me when I'm gone!

I didn't understand this contradiction until I began reading blogs written by other autistic people. Pretty much they all agree that those who receive care get just as tired as those who give care. The only difference is that caregivers can walk away when burnout occurs, caregivees can't. "We learn to try not to ask for more than the bare minimum of what we need," writes Amanda Baggs in her Ballastexistenz blog. Because of the "power imbalances," nonessential needs often go unfulfilled, according to Baggs. Even when she gets frustrated, she's reluctant to say anything because of "possible penalties." "We know that we can't walk away."

Having been enlightened by Ballastexistenz and other blogs, I try to hang around the house and make myself available without being conspicuous. Problem is, Sam resents the fact that he needs lots of assistance with daily living. He depends on prompts when showering or getting dressed, and he requires actual assistance when cooking or cleaning, what little he does. Forget unwanted help. Sometimes after lunch if someone suggests wiping catsup off his face, he'll smear on another layer. Clean that! More than one person has been smacked for cleaning where they shouldn't have been cleaning. He feels belittled when asked to do basic tasks, especially hygiene. "Are you making fun of me?" he'll ask.

Sam resents the pressure to be "normal." To behave "normally." Some days he'll try to pass; other days he won't bother. We might be walking through the local Kroger's looking for something we can't find. Usually Sam will get frustrated after a few minutes, and I'll hear behind me a loud: "WOOOF!" No matter where he happens to be, Sam will often bark when he gets nervous. This can be embarrassing if we're walking through Kroger's or standing in line at the cinema. But, as our favorite Kroger cashier told us recently, "Hey, you guys aren't the only ones who bark here!"

Other autistic people have commented on trying to pass by controlling their behaviors. In her blog Autism Diva explains what happens when autistic people try to "pass for normal." "Passing for normal, smiling when you don't want to smile, suppressing a desire to flap or perseverate ... helps in some situations to get along with normal people, but it shifts the stress to elsewhere in the psyche because one isn't allowed to be one's self," she writes.

My work presents special problems. Sam likes to be left alone for a couple of hours each day, but when I go to work a couple of hours becomes five or six. The result: resentment. He resents me for not being there for him. I resent him for making my life difficult. Some days, pressed for time on a morning when I should already be at work, I'll get overly frustrated and snap, "I hate my life!" If he's feeling frisky, Sam might respond: "Got an issue? Grab a tissue," a line from *Austin Powers: Goldmember.* Or he might quote a line from a long-forgotten Bruce Willis movie: "Wanh! Wanh! Call a wanhmbulance!"

Note: Sam collects popular culture tidbits the way other young men collect baseball cards or beer bottles. No matter the situation, he has a line from a song or a movie at the tip of his tongue. Touché.

Here I have to defend myself. Who wouldn't be resentful when just being able to get free from home responsibilities long enough to go to work (and stay there) becomes a major issue? Too many times I've been in the middle of an important faculty meeting only to have my damn cell phone go off in my pocket. When you're life is as stressed as mine, the initial shock of a vibrating phone feels like a jolt of electricity from a taser gun. Let's face it, I'm shell-shocked. "Did you give Sam his meds before you left?" Or: "Come home! Sam's out of control! He's banging his head against the wall!"

Sam gets a real kick out of calling me during office hours, when I'm meeting with students. "Who are you talking to?" he'll ask. "Can I talk to them?" Or he might call to ask if I saw any fire trucks on my way to work, or to ask what the weather is like on campus. Lately he's been calling to check on my colleague, Jenny, two offices down. He likes to ask Jenny what she's had for lunch that day. Or he wants to ask for the umpteenth time about her favorite pizza restaurant, hoping this time she'll say Uno's, his favorite. Sometimes he'll try to convince her to listen to the latest rap music. He's been known to talk with Jenny while I meet with a student.

Even worse is when Sam calls while I'm teaching. Try teaching a class tethered to a cell phone. I say tethered because, unlike most everybody else in the world, I carry a cell phone out of necessity (to be in touch with whoever's with Sam) rather than choice. If I had a choice, I'd toss the phone in the nearest trash bin. Just this past quarter I was teaching a News Writing and Reporting class in a computer lab, standing at the front of the classroom talking to my students when I heard the dreaded ring and felt the taser sting my leg. I jumped back a step before realizing it was only the phone and not the campus police come to arrest me for some transgression. Parking?

On this particular day I didn't face an emergency. Lucky me.

No need to rush home or meet them at the hospital. "Sam can't find his CD player," my wife said. "Do you know where he put it?"

I explained the situation to my students and apologized for the interruption. As it turned out, I needn't have worried, because the students weren't paying attention anyway. We were supposed to be collectively writing a news story, but most of the students were checking their e-mail, text-messaging on their cell phones, or playing online poker.

Sometimes resentment rears its ugly head in other ways at work. Some of my colleagues resent me for not being around much. I, in turn, resent them for not understanding my situation. For not understanding that when one member of a family is disabled, the entire family becomes (in a sense) disabled.

Occasionally when I'm even more stressed than usual, say when Sam is in the hospital on a day I'm supposed to be teaching, I might have a momentary bout of self-pity. I might feel like I'm the only person who has these problems, even though I know this is not the case. Disability touches everyone sooner or later. Fact is, we will all become disabled if we live long enough. I'm aware of that, and yet it's so easy to play the martyr.

What I need in those moments is for Sam to pipe up with: "Wanh! Wanh! Call a wanhmbulance!"

Usually, though, teaching provides an antidote to self-pity because my university, like most public universities, has recently experienced a dramatic increase in the number of disabled students enrolling. Many of the disabled students who take classes in my department (English) tend to end up my classes. They know about my disability rights advocacy and my work in the academic field of Disability Studies. More to the point, they know I'll be sympathetic. How could I not be, given my experience with Sam? I encourage them to register with the university Disability Services office so that they'll be legally protected. Once registered, they must be provided with reasonable accommodations: more time for tests, aides who take notes, large-print class materials, whatever they need.

As an illustration of how disability enters the classroom, let me tell you about one particular class a few years back. On this day I'd spent the morning with Sam, who happened to be in the hospital, and then driven to campus to teach an afternoon creative nonfiction workshop that enrolled both seniors and graduate students. Several students had asked to present that day, so we didn't waste any time on preliminaries. Mike went first, presenting a funny essay on motorcycles and teenage rebellion. Everyone loved it, especially me, having just come from the psych ward at the university hospital, not exactly a fun place to spend time. I needed a dose of humor, in lieu of a stiff drink. Unfortunately, after Mike the workshop took a turn toward the morose. The next reader plodded through a sad, overly sentimental memoir of a favorite childhood tree that died and had to be cut down about the same time the parents divorced. It was like the air had suddenly gone out of the room.

Now Sarah, a graduate student, reads from her account of her twin sister's death from meningitis a year earlier. She stops occasionally to wipe her eyes and regain her composure. Some students are beginning to fidget at their desks. One guy in back leaves the room, returning a few minutes later to find Sarah still struggling to get through her reading. For a moment I think he's going to scream STOP! and rip her manuscript to shreds the way that John Belushi smashed the earnest folk singer's guitar in the movie *Animal House*.

I'm troubled by the long faces, by the heavy burden of grief that's come over the class. I'm worried especially about my students with disabilities. I notice Selena, who has frequent panic attacks, beginning to rock back and forth while hugging herself tightly with both arms. Beth, a young woman with epilepsy, has closed her eyes and is resting her head on the desk. Not a good sign.

Soon Sarah begins to sob at the front table, unable to continue reading. Visibly shaken by the emotion released in the room, Beth struggles to stand up, but she's unsteady on her feet. She asks Eric, an older nontraditional student, if he will help her out of the room. I see what's about to happen and quickly follow them into the hallway. Eric and I ease Beth onto a bench and then to the floor as she begins to have a grand mal seizure. Soon Carol, a student with a background in nursing, comes out to help. I tell Eric to stay with the class while Carol and I hold Beth, making sure she doesn't hurt herself. As soon as she can talk she asks for her meds, which we find in her backpack. But the meds don't stop the convulsions. After 10 minutes, beginning to worry, I call 911 and ask for help. Then I call Beth's roommate, whose name and telephone number Beth had given me just in case this would happen during class.

"Okay. I guess I could come down," the roommate says, sounding tentative.

"Actually, why don't you meet us in the emergency room. The paramedics are on their way."

By this time most of the other students have come out into the hallway. There's not much I can do but dismiss class.

Carol and Eric say they'll stay with Beth until the paramedics arrive, so I go back into the classroom to check on Sarah.

Sarah hasn't moved. She's still sitting at the front table holding the loose pages that together tell the tragedy of her sister's death. To my great surprise, she's all smiles.

"I'm really sorry," Sarah says, a slight young woman with short blond hair and watery blue eyes who looks to be about 13 years old. "I just really needed to write about my sister ... to get it out. I feel much better now."

"No need to feel sorry. You didn't know."

Back in the hallway, I'm just in time for the paramedics, who lift Beth and her backpack onto a stretcher. She looks at me, expecting me to say something. What?

"Okay then," I say. "I'll see you at the hospital." I figured I would stop at the Emergency Room first, then go up to Sam's floor.

I think about this class whenever I'm tempted to feel self-pity or resentment, whenever I need to remind myself that disability is a public, not a personal matter.

Chapter 22

Community

People in my town are used to seeing Sam and I together. So if I'm out running errands without him, people notice his absence. "Where's Sam?" I hear it everywhere.

When I get home, I'll often find Sam standing in the driveway talking to our neighbors. We're fortunate to live on a quiet street where pretty much everyone knows and accepts Sam. Most of our immediate neighbors are either retired or stay-at-home spouses, which means they're home every day to chat with Sam. Or to help him, in the event of an emergency.

I might find Sam outside matching wits with Roger next door. Sam loves to give Roger a hard time. "Hey, Roger, are you keeping your nose clean?" he'll ask.

Or: "Hey, Roger, you'll never guess where I saw you last night ... on American's Most Wanted!"

For his part, Roger will joke with Sam about his bad taste in music or his bad diet (even though, much to Sam's delight, Roger goes to Uno's almost as often as Sam does).

Afterwards, Sam will say, "I'm just messing with you."

"Me, too," Roger will say.

When Roger's not available, Sam will talk to Cindy across the street about her dog, a goofy looking beagle. Or he'll talk to Scott next door about his lawn, which he keeps meticulously coiffed. And so on down the street.

Sam loves his neighborhood — and his neighbors. His situation would be perfect if only there were some stores or restaurants within walking distance. As it is, Sam has to catch a ride with me or one of his other companions if he wants to go anywhere. If and when we move, it will have to be somewhere Sam can get around by foot. He's a powerful walker.

Even more than most people, Sam needs a community. He longs for connection, a sense of belonging. That's why he attaches himself one-on-one to whomever he's with. And that's why he tries so hard to strike up conversations and make friends. Without a defined place in the world, he feels lost, free-floating, without moorings or destination. Alone.

Our neighbors understand Sam's need for connection. They go out of their way to include him in neighborhood parties and other events. Inclusion helps Sam feel better about himself. But you know what, inclusion is also good for the neighbors, and good for the larger community. Fact is, the community also gains in subtle, intangible ways from helping and supporting people who need a little extra assistance. It's hard to make this argument without sounding sentimental, which I'm not. But here goes.

In a culture that routinely dumps the ill, the infirm, and the elderly in institutions of one kind or another, it's rare that a person has the deeply humanizing experience of caring for someone who's needy. Let's face it, some people have greater need for care and assistance than others. But so what? Other people have greater need for other kinds of things, material wealth or whatever. Is needing help less worthy than needing a BMW? I don't think so.

Caring for someone with a disability is deeply humanizing because it reaffirms a common humanity. Not only that, but such care involves the recognition that all of us, if we live long enough, will become disabled; that all of us, even if we're temporarily able-bodied, rely on countless others every day of our lives. The peculiarly American myth of the autonomous individual has made it more difficult to see the social network that enables (or disables) all of us. You might say it's a case of not seeing the forest for the trees.

Let me clarify something I said earlier. When I say Sam needs a community, I don't mean to suggest that there's only one community. There are smaller social networks within the larger community. For example, Sam attended a wonderfully inclusive neighborhood elementary school, where his class became his immediate community.

Later Sam joined a local T-Ball team that played in the Challenger Division of Little League. For nearly 10 years, Sam's team, the mighty Lakota Indians, became his summer community. Except that Sam's version of T-Ball differed from that of his teammates. Sam played a talking game. He would whack the ball, then trot around the bases asking the puzzled members of the opposing team questions about the weather. Much the same happened when Sam's team took the field. Usually Sam would ignore the balls hit toward him. If he did decide to field a ball, it was because he wanted to throw or carry it to a particular teammate, so that the two of them could chat about the weather. For Sam, baseball was just another form of conversation.

Later still Sam joined a social club, where twice a month he went on outings, either social or service (giving back to the community). For many years his social club became another of his overlapping communities.

Eventually, though, Sam became an adult. He graduated from elementary school, outgrew T-Ball, and moved on from his social club. And here's the rub. Finding community as a disabled adult is not an easy thing to do. Some of Sam's old friends still belong to social clubs or churches, but Sam hasn't chosen to join them. That leaves Sam with limited options.

I don't want to suggest that Sam doesn't work hard to establish community. He does. He's cultivated relationships with all of our immediate neighbors. In addition, Sam has established deep friendships with his three other companions. He's become part of their families. On outings they'll often take him to their homes, including him in their private lives.

Still, I worry about the future. Even though Sam has a limited community now, he's really in a holding pattern. Increasingly, he refuses to explore new possibilities or to make new friends. He wants his life to remain the same, which as we all know is impossible.

Adulthood marks a dangerous transition for autistic and disabled people. It's infinitely more difficult to establish connection and find a place in the world when you're an adult with distinctly different behaviors and habits instead of a cute and cuddly child. Barking, grabbing, and other autistic behaviors might be overlooked in a child, but not in an adult. Just ask Sam.

Of course, place affects the difficulty of the transition. Let's face it, some social environments are more accepting of difference than others. Location can make a huge difference in whether an autistic person succeeds or fails to establish community. Here's Autism Diva on this subject: "It seems to Autism Diva that there are autistics who try hard to get along in social situations and are very aware of how they fail. Many are aided in gaining a keen awareness of their social failures by people telling them that they are geeks, losers and weirdos and generally that they should 'get lost.'" Other autistic people might be as socially inept but are less aware of their social awkwardness and, as a consequence, will continue to interact with people in spite of whatever the general reaction to them is.

What's the difference in the two groups? Autism Diva explains: "One supposes that part of the difference between the two groups has to do with the kinds of people that are in the immediate social milieu and how much pressure there is on the autistic person to perform social behaviors in an absolutely 'standard' way."

Partly in response to being socially ostracized, autistic people have created their own cyber community. Websites like Autism Hub and Autism-Vox connect autistic people and allow them to comment on each other's blogs and posts. More autistic bloggers appear every year, joining the ongoing discussions. The result: an interactive network buzzing with energy and ideas and sometimes fierce disagreements. After reading a few of these exchanges, it should be clear to everyone that it's no longer appropriate to talk about autism without including autistic voices.

But a cyber community can't completely replace an actual

community. The sad fact remains that today too many autistic adults are placed, against their will, in group homes and institutions. Those fortunate enough to live semi-independently in their communities require services, which are often hard to obtain. There's the sticking point. For autistic adults to have semi-independent lives in their communities, they need companions and assistants to help with cleaning, cooking, shopping, getting to doctors appointments, and the like. And where do autistic adults find these services? Who pays for them?

Consider Sam. Even though he's eligible for a Medicaid waiver to pay for such services and service providers, his county MRDD doesn't have enough waivers allotted by the state for all who need them. MRDD pays for one of his companions; we pay for the other two. The only additional assistance Sam receives is a small monthly SSI check from the federal government and state Medicaid, which he has never used, because so far our health insurance has covered him and also because the state-selected Medicaid HMO doesn't include the specialists he needs.

So what happens when we retire and suddenly Sam has to live on $400 a month and rely on state medical coverage that doesn't provide neurosurgeons for his shunt or psychiatrists for his mood disorder? You see the problem.

Community depends on services. Without services, there is no community, especially for autistic and disabled people. For anyone really, since all of us depend on services of one kind or another, as I have argued in an earlier chapter.

Without services, and without community, bad things happen to autistic people. Sometimes even living with parents (or other family members) is not the ideal situation. If you spend much time in the autistic blogosphere, you encounter dozens of posts about autistic children who have been murdered by so-called "overburdened" parents who decided to "terminate" the lives of their children. Katherine McCarron, Marcus Fiesel, Alison Davis, Christopher DeGroot, Ulysses Stable, to name only some of the more recently murdered children. On their websites the bloggers maintain a running roll call of the dead, a cyber requiem that continues, year after year, murdered child after murdered child.

Last August Marcus Fiesel was murdered not far from where I live. A 3-year-old with behavior issues, Marcus' foster parents (and their live-in girlfriend) pinned his arms behind his back, wrapped him in a blanket, bound him with packing tape, and locked him in a 5 × 7 foot closet while they attended a two-day family reunion across the Ohio River in Kentucky. Temperatures in the closet reached well over 100 degrees, according to authorities.

When the foster parents and their girlfriend returned two days later, they found Marcus dead. They placed the body in a cardboard box and took it to an abandoned chimney in rural Ohio. After dousing Marcus with gasoline, they incinerated his body and then dumped the remains in the Ohio River. Such was the short, brutalized life of Marcus Fiesel.

In the end, services and community are even more important than parents. For quality of life. For life itself.

Joel Smith addresses this quality-of-life issue in a recent post on his NTs Are Weird blog. "I'm saddened as I see many in my community (that is, autistic people) who are living horrid lives," he writes. "We are abused, ignored, neglected, rejected, murdered, hated, victimized, medicated, and marginalized."

Smith goes on to argue that autistic people, whatever their level of ability, can lead happy lives. Their happiness depends not on what they can or can't do, but on how they are treated by the people around them. Autistic people require only "a safe environment with the proper supports," where they can be themselves, find their desired level of human companionship, and have a way of contributing to the world.

So, again, we come back to services and community. A safe environment with the proper supports. Accommodations.

In her blog of the same name, Aspie Bird reflects specifically on "Autists and Housing Needs." Good housing "counts double for people with autism," she writes, then goes on to list the kinds of living arrangements preferred by most autistic people. First, living at home with the help of parents and external support workers. Second, living in a supported home. Third, living alone and independently, with external support when needed. And fourth, living independently with the help of a partner, with external support when needed.

Though Aspie Bird has lived in her own apartment for about 10 years, she admits that living independently can be very stressful during the more difficult periods of life. Being independent comes with a price. "Looking back on all those often lonely years I wonder if I would like to keep on living on like this. All these years I often felt lonely and got very stressed. I missed social contacts!" she writes. "When I continue to live on my own I might miss a lot of fun and social things the people who live in a shared house might have."

She concludes: "I wonder if there would be a way of living possible to have the best of two worlds: Support, extra care, company from others and freedom to live on one's own. I have a dream of being able to live with some other adults with ASD together in a kind of community. Not specific group living but each person with their own home and responsibility. Like a collection of individuals who can find each other's company when needed/ appreciated."

A dream?

Well, I confess to a similar dream. I dream that one day Sam will live in an inclusive community, where he will be valued for who he is, not judged for what he's not.

My idea of the ideal living situation for Sam would be an apartment or a condo in some kind of complex that would include people of varying ages and abilities, including (of course) other autistic people. He might live by himself or with a partner, someone with whom he's "mutual" as Sam likes to say. Male, female, gay or straight, it doesn't matter to me. Just so he's happy.

A place where Sam will never be lonely or abandoned. Where he will never be abused like Marcus Fiesel and so many others.

I imagine a nearby village or city centre, within walking distance, with shops and stores, restaurants and cinemas. I see parks, walking trails, and a recreation center. I see on-site medical and dental care.

For Sam, I see assistants who will come at appointed hours each day to help with daily living activities. Whatever he needs.

Imagine.

Chapter 23

Looking for Autism Pride Day

This year I determined to celebrate Autism Pride Day, an annual event held on June 18. I had visions of a zany, rollicking, barking parade ending up downtown on Fountain Square. I mean, every year parades march through downtown to mark St. Patrick's Day, Columbus Day, Gay Pride Day, and what have you, so why not Autism Pride Day?

Imagine my disappointment when I contacted the Autism Society of Greater Cincinnati and discovered that no downtown parade had been scheduled. In fact, ASGC hadn't planned any events related to Autism Pride Day. Instead, during the month of June, they'd organized the second annual "Chicken and Booze Golf Outing for Autism" and the fourth annual "Bowling for Autism." No kidding. I'm not making this up, as Dave Barry likes to say.

Believe me, I have nothing whatsoever against golf or booze, but golfing and boozing don't seem like the most appropriate ways to celebrate neurodiversity. Bowling might be a little better, but it's not exactly what I had in mind.

For a moment I pondered asking Tim, one of the team leaders at Sam's former social club, to pull together his autistic troops and march on downtown. Or at least organize another outing to the riverfront Hooters, *déjà vu.*

No, that wouldn't do either, although Hooters and neurodiversity seemed a closer match.

But let's forget golfing, boozing, and bowling. After all, the idea behind Autism Pride Day is to celebrate neurodiversity, especially the neurodiversity of people living on the autism spectrum. Initiated by Aspies for Freedom, the event debuted in 2005 with private celebrations worldwide and a central celebration organized in Brasilia, capital of Brazil. According to the Aspies for Freedom website, the goals of Autism Pride Day include "promoting the basic human rights of autistics and finding a valued home for their individual voice and talents." The event is also intended to educate the general public on the "positive aspects [of autism] that can be celebrated."

Sounds good, so why aren't we celebrating?

To be fair, the large, non-autistic advocacy organizations are not alone in their reluctance to get involved in Autism Pride Day. There's also ambivalence within the autistic community itself on whether (and how best) to celebrate the event.

On the second annual Autism Pride Day (2006), Joseph commented on this ambivalence in his Natural Variation blog. He tried to clarify some of the issues raised by the event. "Not surprisingly, I get the feeling that we have not come to terms with what 'autistic pride' should be about," he writes.

He draws parallels with other Pride movements: Gay Pride, Black Pride, Disability Pride, and Deaf Pride. Then, in the context of these other movements, he offers his own definition of the premises underlying autistic pride:

(1) That autistic people should be proud, not ashamed of who they are;

(2) That neurological diversity is both positive and a necessary part of human life;

(3) That autism is "inherent and pervasive" and cannot be removed without also destroying the autistic person;

(4) That autistic people have worth and are valuable members of society;

(5) That autistic people should not be forced to act "normal"; and

(6) That efforts aimed at curing, defeating and exterminating autistic people are "inherently misguided."

He ends by saying, "Finally, I want to emphasize that pride is the opposite of shame. We should not be ashamed of who we are. We should not be ashamed of what others perceive as quirks or shortcomings. There is no reason to be ashamed of hand-flapping, fidgeting, rocking and so on."

No one makes the case better than the Autistic Bitch from Hell in a scathing post debunking those who would shame autistic people. Her post also dates from 2006, the second year that Autism Pride Day was celebrated. She begins by explaining why the event is called Autism Pride Day, so that the curebies and other nay-sayers who don't feel autism is something to celebrate might achieve a glimmer of understanding. Fact is, autistic people are proud of their identity and, just like the members of any other "minority group," want to express pride in their identity and demand recognition and respect from society.

"Excuuuuse us if we're being politically incorrect by not calling this event 'a day for people with an unmentionable abnormality to whisper about,'" she writes.

I couldn't agree more. No autistic or disabled person should ever feel ashamed, or be made to feel ashamed by insensitive, misguided neuro-typicals. Shame can be a powerful and debilitating emotion. I know this from watching Sam's ongoing battle with low self-esteem. Sam still feels badly about himself when he notices people looking at him in a certain way. The HEY, LOOK AT THE FREAK WITH CATSUP ON HIS FACE look.

Even at the age of 26, Sam sees himself in the way other people react to him. For Sam, watching their reactions is like looking in a mirror. He's especially sensitive about eating and toileting mishaps. Nothing embarrasses him more than having to change clothes before leaving on one of his outings. He feels demeaned, belittled, ashamed, and sometimes angry.

"Don't be embarrassed," I'll say when he has to change clothes. "Everybody has accidents. It's no big deal."

"Do you have accidents?" Sam asks.

"You bet!" I'll say, and then I tell him about some of my mishaps.

Sam listens to my stories, but sometimes it's hard for him to overcome what he's learned to see as his shortcomings, his failings. He's internalized the reactions of other people. Now he has to un-internalize them.

Lately Sam has made progress, though. He's more resilient, more independent, more able to ignore the reactions of other people, to toss off whatever negativity he encounters.

Pride, not shame. That's the message of Autism Pride Day. It's a message that Sam understands intuitively. From the time he was a toddler, he responded only to positive feedback. He wants to hear positive things about himself and his life.

So, yes, we were definitely ready to celebrate autistic pride, if only we could find a parade, a march, a love-in, something.

But we didn't.

To make a long story short, we ended up going for a long walk and having a heartfelt, father and son conversation. We followed our regular walking trail for a mile or so, then sat down on a bench overlooking a wetland pond, where a few ducks were gliding peacefully across the surface of the pond. No one else was on the trail that morning, just the two of us and the ducks.

"Sam, what are you most proud of?" I asked him finally, after a long silence.

He cocked his head back and to the left, so as to get a good look at me. "Why do you want to know?"

I reminded him it was Autism Pride Day.

After a few moments, he turned to me and said, "I'm proud of everything. I'm proud that I'm twenty-six. That I've grown up. Aren't you proud of me?"

"Of course I'm proud of you," I said. "You know I'm proud of you."

He nodded, gently rocking his head from side to side, lost in thought.

"But why are you proud of me?"

"For lots of reasons. Your intelligence ... your sense of humor ... your language skills ... your ability to make friends ... your spirit," I said, rattling off a list of his more endearing attributes.

Apparently, though, I'd omitted one thing he wanted me to mention.

"What about how far I've come?"

"AND how far you've come!" I said.

Now Sam was satisfied with my answer. We didn't have to elaborate; both of us knew what he'd come though to get here, the surgeries and the hospitalizations. We shared an understanding of all that was implied but not spoken.

Sitting there with Sam, reminiscing about how far he'd come, my mind drifted back in time, back to when Sam was in the sixth grade, before the rap music and the terrible high school years, before the meltdowns and the psych hospitalizations, back to the memory of one sweet day that seems to me now like a metaphor for the possibility of inclusion and acceptance.

Back then, Sam was a bright, eager student who looked forward to going to school. On this particular afternoon he wanted to leave early for his school's Family Night. That year, as an extra attraction, the PTA had added a karaoke show to the annual spaghetti dinner, and Sam wanted to check it out.

So we're among the first to arrive in the school cafeteria, decked out in blue and white tablecloths. The teachers, parents, and cafeteria workers all say hello to Sam. Sam pretends not to notice, but my wife and I see the big smile on his face as he carries his tray over to one of the lunch tables and begins eating his chocolate cupcake first. Everyone knows Sam.

By the time we finish our dinner, the people from Sound Productions have set up their karaoke machine on the stage in the rear of the cafeteria. Speakers, stand-up microphone, and video prompter, all tested and ready for action.

When one of the workers comes to our table distributing lists of songs available, Sam asks, "Do we have to sing?" The man laughs and says, "Only if you want to."

Sam ignores him, scouring the song titles for some of his favorites of the moment. No R.E.M. or Talking Heads, but he does find the Beatles and Willie Nelson. Close enough.

Meanwhile, the karaoke people do all the work. They take turns singing on stage, everything from Garth Brooks to Johnny Mathis. Still no requests from the audience, a subdued crowd of curious but shy kids, accompanied by parents who huddle over their plates pretending to be invisible.

But not Sam. He finds a song he likes, "Georgia on My Mind," and asks us to write it down on a slip of paper. Gritting her teeth, Cindy takes the note up to the stage.

"Hey — here's a request," the speakers blare. "From Sam Wilson. He wants to hear 'Georgia on My Mind.' Do you want to sing it, Sam?"

And before we can blink an eye, our eager 13-year-old takes off. He rambles awkwardly through the maze of tables, exactly as he would walk to his classroom or anywhere else. Maybe he has to be helped up on stage, but no matter. When he gets that microphone in his hands and the music kicks in, there's Sam rocking from side to side, crooning out the words to "Georgia on My Mind." A jazz version, a la Ray Charles, with a few extra howls and screams thrown in for effect. He doesn't miss a beat.

The karaoke people can't believe the performance. Neither can the audience. The parents give Sam a big hand as he finishes the song and starts hamming it up for everyone to see, doing a few dance steps for an encore.

After Sam breaks the ice, other kids rush to the stage wanting to sing. And Sam? He's off looking for something else to do.

"Sam, that was great!" the assistant principal tells him on his way out of the cafeteria. "I'm going to tell your teacher tomorrow morning. She'll be sorry she couldn't come tonight."

"Okay," Sam says over his shoulder. And then he's gone, back for another chocolate cupcake, amid congratulations all around.

Classic Sam.

The karaoke performance was Sam at his absolute best. But it didn't happen by accident. He was able to shine because in his elementary school, especially fifth and sixth grades, he was accepted as part of the group. Not only accepted, but valued because of his intelligence and his great enthusiasm for life. He was encouraged to be himself, enabled in a way that allowed him to thrive. At one point during the previous year his teachers asked him to teach a meteorological unit in his science class. And Sam did! We still have the video his teachers made of Sam sitting in front of the class, swiveling his chair and rocking his head back and forth, answering weather questions from the other students.

Sam's experience that year embodies my hope for his future. I want what he wants: a place where he feels comfortable, where he's accepted and valued for the wonderfully distinct person he's become. A place where he can feel proud of himself; proud of how far he's come, as he likes to say. A place where autistic pride isn't relegated to one day per year but celebrated 24/7, 365 days of the year. A place where there's no shame in being different, only pride.

When we finally resumed our walk, turning toward home, I asked Sam about that night. "Do you remember when you sang karaoke at Heritage Elementary? In sixth grade?"

"Yeah, that was back in the DAY, before I got eaten up by rap," he said happily. "I was cool that night."

I agreed. "Very cool."

We'd taken only a few steps before he added, "I think I'm even cooler now."

"Absolutely," I said. "Absolutely."

Sources

Listed in order of appearance.

PREFACE

Autism Diva, http://autismdiva.blogspot.com/
Amanda Baggs, Ballastexistenz, http://ballastexistenz.autistics.org/
Elmindreda, http://elmindreda.blogspot.com/
Autistic Bitch from Hell, Whose Planet Is It Anyway? Aug. 22, 2006, http://autistic
    bfh.blogspot.com/

CHAPTER 2

Centers for Disease Control, "Prevalence of the Autism Spectrum Disorders (ASDs)
    in Multiple Areas of the United States, 2000 and 2002," http://www.cdc.gov/
Autism Society of America, http://www.autism-society.org
Autism Speaks, http://www.autismspeaks.org
Centers for Disease Control, http://www.cdc.gov/ncbddd/autism
Center for the Study of Autism, http://autism.org/contents
Diagnostic and Statistical Manual of Mental Disorders, American Psychiatric
    Association, p. 69–70. Criteria for diagnosing "Autistic Disorder" can be found
    on the CDC website, http://www.cdc.gov/ncbdd/autism/overview_diagnostic_
    criteria.htm
Temple Grandin, "An Inside View of Autism," http://autism.org/temple/inside.html
Autism Network International, http://ani.autistics.org
Aspies for Freedom, http://www.aspiesforfreedom.com
Autism Vox, http://autismvox.com
Autistics.Org, http://www.autistics.org
Autism Hub, http://www.autism-hub.co.uk/
Autism Diva, Feb. 7, 2007, http://autismdiva.blogspot.com
Kassiane Montana, Rett Devil, Jan. 14, 2007, http://rettdevil.blogspot.com/
Michelle Dawson, Autism Crisis, Oct. 28, 2006, http://autismcrisis.blogspot.com

Venturra33, http://ventura33.com/neurodiversity
Amanda Baggs, http://gettingthetruthout.org

CHAPTER 3

Letter and CCDD report to author dated Oct. 18, 1985.
Zilari, Processing in Parts, Feb. 6, 2007, http://partprocessing.blogspot.com
ADA Homepage, http://usdoj.gov/crt/ada/adahtml
Eugenics Archive, http://www.eugenicsarchive.org
Joel Smith, NTs Are Weird, Feb. 14, 2007, http://thiswayoflife.org/blog
Donna Williams, *Nobody Nowhere: The Extraordinary Autobiography of an Autistic*,
    p. 46.
Letter from CCDD to author dated April 25, 1986.

CHAPTER 4

Donna Williams, *Nobody Nowhere: The Extraordinary Autobiography of an Autistic*,
    p. 213.
Kassiane Montana, Rett Devil, June 3, 2006, http://rettdevil.blogspot.com
Elmindreda, Nov. 9, 2005, http://elmindreda.blogspot.com
Michele Dawson, Autism Crisis, Dec. 3, 2006, http://autismcrisis.blogspot.com
Sue Rubin, "Killing Autism Is a Constant Battle," http://suedweb.syr.edu/thefci/4-1
    rub2.htm

CHAPTER 5

Joel Smith, NTs Are Weird, Oct. 22, 2006, http://thiswayoflife.org/blog
Andrea, Andrea's Buzzing About, Feb. 21, 2007, http://qw88nb88.wordpress.com
Temple Grandin, "An Inside View of Autism," Center for the Study of Autism,
    http://www.autism.org/temple/inside.html
Temple Grandin, "My Experiences with Visual Thinking, Sensory Problems, and
    Communication Difficulties," Center for the Study of Autism, http://www.
    autism.org/temple/visual.html

CHAPTER 7

Elmindreda, Feb, 13, 2006, http://elmindreda.blogspot.com
Lori Berkowitz, LBnuke. June 5, 2006, http://lbnuke.com
Mr. Nickelpie, Letter to author, Dec. 19, 2001.
Autistic Bitch from Hell, Whose Planet Is It Anyway? Dec. 3, 2006, http://autistic
    bfh.blogspot.com

Daniel Passantino, "Autism on Campus: The Other Diversity," Feb. 25, 2007, http://www.cnn.com

CHAPTER 8

Amanda Baggs, Ballastexistenz, Jan. 17, 2007, http://ballastexistenz.autistics.org
Sue Rubin, "Killing Autism Is a Constant Battle," http://suedweb.syr.edu/thefci/4-1 rub2.htm
Donna Williams, *Nobody Nowhere: The Extraordinary Autobiography of an Autistic*, p. 213.
Michelle Dawson, Autism Crisis, Dec. 3, 2006, http://autismcrisis.blogspot.com
Amanda Baggs, Ballastexistenz, May 16, 2006, http://ballastexistenz.autistics.org

CHAPTER 9

Warren Faidley. *Storm Chaser*. VHS. Atlanta: The Weather Channel, 1996.
Warren Faidley, *Storm Chaser: In Pursuit of Untamed Skies*. Atlanta: The Weather Channel, 1996.
Warren Faidley, http://www.stormchaser.com
Weatherwise magazine, http://weatherwise.org

CHAPTER 10

Autism Speaks, "Mission," http://www.autismspeaks.org
Cure Autism Now, http://www.cureautismnow.org
Combating Autism Act, President's Statement, http://listserv.access.gpo.gov/cgi-bin
Lisa, Lisa-Jedi, Aug. 3, 2006, http://lisa-jedi.blogspot.com
Autistic Bitch from Hell, Whose Planet Is It Anyway? Dec. 11, 2006, http://autistic bfh.blogspot.com
Ken Garber, "Autism Cause May Reside in Abnormalities at the Synapse," *Science*, pp. 190–91.
President's Council on Bioethics, *Beyond Therapy: Biotechnology and the Pursuit of Perfection* (later changed to *Happiness*), Chapter 2, "Better Children," 2003, http://www.bioethics.gov/reports/beyondtherapy
Joseph, Natural Variation, March 31, 2006, http://autismnaturalvariation.blogspot.com/
Sue Rubin, "Acceptance Versus Cure," Feb. 15, 2007, http://www.cnn.com/cnn/programs/presents/shows/autism.world/notebooks/sue/notebook
Cal Montgomery, "Defining Autistic Lives," http://www.raggededgemagazine.com/reviews/ckmontrubin0605.html
Autistic Bitch from Hell, Whose Planet Is It Anyway? Jan. 3, 2007. http://autistic bfh.blogspot.com

CHAPTER 11

Joel Smith, NTs Are Weird, Sept. 13, 2006, http://thiswayoflife.org/blog
Spokette, Misadventures from a Different Perspective, Aug. 30, 2006, http://spokette.blogspot.com

CHAPTER 12

Jane Gross, "For Siblings of the Autistic, a Burdened Youth," Dec. 10, 2004, http://www.nytimes.com/2004/12/10/health/10siblings.html
Kassiane Montana, Rett Devil, April 5, 2006, http://rettdevil.blogspot.com
Spockette, Misadventures from a Different Perspective, Dec. 11, 2006, http://spockette.blogspot.com

CHAPTER 13

Centers for Disease Control, http://www.cdc.gov/ncbddd/autism
Rich Shull, Pre Rain Man Autism, Jan. 25, 2007, http://prerainmanautism.blogspot.com
Zilari, Processing in Parts, Feb. 6, 2007, http://partprocessing.blogspot.com
Elmindreda, March 11, 2006, http://elmindreda.blogspot.com
Sue Rubin, http://sue-rubin.org
Profile of Amanda Baggs, "Living with Autism in a World Made for Others," http://www.cnn.com/2007/health/02/21/autism.amanda
Amanda Baggs, Ballastexistenz, May 4, 2006, http://ballastexistenz.autistics.org

CHAPTER 14

Leo Kanner, "Autistic Disturbances of Affective Contact," *Nervous Child* 2 (1943): 217–250.
Bruno Bettelheim, *The Empty Fortress: Infantile Autism and the Birth of the Self.* New York: Free Press, 1967.
Simon Baron-Cohen. *Mindblindness.* Cambridge, Mass.: MIT Press, 1995.
Zilari, Processing in Parts, Jan. 31, 2006, http://partprocessing.blogspot.com
Stephen Pinker, *The Blank Slate*, p. 62.
Larry Arnold, Laurentius Rex, Aug, 20 and May 6, 2006, http://laurentius-rex.blogspot.com
Temple Grandin, *Thinking in Pictures and Other Reports from My Life with Autism*, pp. 19, 20, 21, 27–28, 33.
Rich Shull, Pre Rain Man Autism, Sept. 29 and April 8, 2006, http://prerainmanautism.blogspot.com
Chasmatazz, The Art of Understanding, Oct. 24, 2006, http://theartofunderstanding.blogspot.com

Interverbal, Reviews of Autism Statements and Research, Nov. 27, 2006, http://
interverbal.blogspot.com

CHAPTER 15

Amanda Baggs, Ballastexistenz, Jan. 27, 2007, http://ballastexistenz.autistics.org
Lori Berkowitz, LBnuke, March 20, 2007, http://lbnuke.com

CHAPTER 16

Amanda Baggs, Ballastexistenz, June 25, 2006, http://ballastexistenz.autistics.org
Cal Montgomery, "Critic of the Dawn," *Ragged Edge*, Issue 2, 2001, http://www.
raggededgemagazine.com/0501/0501/htm

CHAPTER 17

Chasmatazz, The Art of Understanding, March 1, 2007, http://theartofunderstand
ing.blogspot.com
Zilari, Processing in Parts, Dec. 31, 2006, http://partprocessing.blogspot.com
Jonathan Sebat, et al., "Strong Association of De Novo Copy Number Mutations
with Autism," *Science*, p. 445.
James C. Wilson and Cynthia Lewiecki-Wilson, "Disability, Rhetoric, and the
Body," in *Embodied Rhetorics: Disability in Language and Culture*, p. 14–15.
Elmindreda, Dec. 26, 2005, http://elmindreda.blogspot.com
Joel Smith, NTs Are Weird, Jan. 27, 2007, http://thiswayoflife.org/blog

CHAPTER 18

James W. Trent, Jr., *Inventing the Feeble Mind: A History of Mental Retardation in the
United States*, p. 241.
Pearl S. Buck. *The Child Who Never Grew*. New York: John Day, 1950.
John P. Frank. *My Son's Story*. New York: Alfred A. Knopf, 1952.
Dale Evans Rogers. *Angel Unaware*. Westwood, N.J.: Revell, 1953.
John Hockenberry, *Moving Violations: A Memoir*, pp. 336–7 and 338–9.
Erving Goffman. *Asylum: Essays on the Social Situation of Mental Patients and Other
Inmates*. New York: Doubleday, 1961.

CHAPTER 20

Zilari, Processing in Parts, Aug. 3, 2006, http://partprocessing.blogspot.com
Autistic Bitch from Hell, Whose Planet Is It Anyway? April 4, 2007, http://autistic
bfh.blogspot.com

Cal Montgomery, "Autistics Speak," *Ragged Edge*, Dec. 16, 2005, http://www.ragged
edgemagazine.com
Autistic Bitch from Hell, Whose Planet Is It Anyway? Jan. 2206, http://autisticbfh.
blogspot.com

Chapter 21

Amanda Baggs, Ballastexistenz, May 18, 2006, http://ballastexistenz.autistics.org
Autism Diva, Dec. 17, 2006, http://autismdiva.blogspot.com

Chapter 22

Autism Diva, Feb. 18, 2006, http://autismdiva.blogspot.com
Joel Smith, NTs Are Weird, March 6, 2007, http://thiswayoflife.org/blog
Aspie Bird, Aug. 17, 2006, http://aspie_bird.blogspot.com

Chapter 23

Autism Society of Greater Cincinnati, http://www.autismcincy.org
Aspies for Freedom, http://aspiesforfreedom.com
Joseph, Natural Variation, June 18, 2006, http://autismnaturalvariation.blogspot.
com
Autistic Bitch from Hell, Whose Planet Is It Anyway? May 3, 2006, http://autistic
bfh.blogspot.com

Bibliography

Baron-Cohen, Simon. *Mindblindness*. Cambridge, Mass.: MIT Press, 1995.
Bettelheim, Bruno. *The Empty Fortress: Infantile Autism and the Birth of the Self.* New York: Free Press, 1967.
Buck, Pearl S. *The Child Who Never Grew*. New York: John Day, 1950.
Diagnostic and Statistical Manual of Mental Disorders. Washington, D.C.: American Psychiatric Association, 2000.
Faidley, Warren. *Storm Chaser: In Pursuit of Untamed Skies*. Atlanta: The Weather Channel: 1996.
Frank, John P. *My Son's Story*. New York: Alfred A. Knopf, 1952.
Garber, Ken. "Autism's Cause May Reside in Abnormalities at the Synapse." *Science*, Vol. 317, No. 5835 (July 13, 2007): 190-91.
Goffman, Erving. *Asylum: Essays on the Social Situation of Mental Patients and Other Inmates*. New York: Doubleday, 1961.
Grandin, Temple. *Thinking in Pictures and Other Reports from My Life with Autism*. New York: Doubleday, 1995.
Haddon, Mark. *The Curious Incident of the Dog in the Night-Time*. New York: Doubleday, 2003.
Hockenberry, John. *Moving Violations: A Memoir*. New York: Hyperion, 1995.
Kanner, Leo. "Autistic Disturbances of Affective Contact." *Nervous Child* 2 (1943): 217-250.
Newport, Jerry, Mary Newport, and Johnny Dodd. *Mozart and the Whale*. New York: Touchstone, 2007.
Pinker, Stephen. *The Blank Slate*. London: Penguin, 2002.
Rogers, Dale Evans. *Angel Unaware*. Westwood, N.J.: Revell, 1953.
Rubin, Sue. "Killing Autism Is a Constant Battle." *Facilitated Communication Digest*, Vol. 4, No. 1 (Nov. 1995).
Savarese, Ralph. *Reasonable People: A Memoir of Autism and Adoption*. New York: Other Press, 2007.
Sebat, Jonathan, et al. "Strong Association of De Novo Copy Number Mutations with Autism." *Science*, Vol. 316, No. 5823 (April 20, 2007): 445-9.
Tammet, David. *Born on a Blue Day: Inside the Extraordinary Mind of an Autistic Savant*. New York: Free Press, 2007.
Trent, James W., Jr. *Inventing the Feeble Mind: A History of Mental Retardation in the United States*. Berkeley: University of California Press, 1994.

Williams, Donna. *Nobody Nowhere: The Extraordinary Autobiography of an Autistic.* New York: Times Books, 1992.

Wilson, James C., and Cynthia Lewiecki-Wilson. "Disability, Rhetoric, and the Body," in *Embodied Rhetorics: Disability in Language and Culture.* Carbondale: Southern Illinois University Press, 2001, p. 1-24.

Index